Endorsements

The following pages of this book will help you discover foundational truths about what it means to be a follower of Jesus. Gene and Lauren have developed a great resource that will help new believers start their journey with an understanding of their true identity in Christ and the knowledge of how to partner with Jesus in supernatural ways. Following Jesus is a lifestyle full of freedom, empowerment, and loving encounters with God that will propel you into the purpose for which you were created. Learning to follow Jesus takes you step by step through key elements that puts new believers and long-time followers of Jesus on the fast track to understanding their pivotal role in the kingdom of God. But this is more than a book, it is the practical application that Gene and Lauren applied to their ministry in Washington D.C. to bring freedom to entire neighborhoods. Everything is better when you are following Jesus!

Georgian Banov, president and co-founder of Global Celebration and GCSSM Online School, author, Joy! God's Secret Weapon for Every Believer

The very first moments I met Gene and Lauren over lunch in Washington D.C., I knew they were the kind of people that everyone should meet. Full of compassion, Holy Spirit gifting, characters full of depth and honesty, coupled with a sharp wit and so much fun to be with. Time spent with Gene and Lauren is time well spent and one is richer as a result of being in their company. They bring all of this and more from their treasured lives into this exciting new book on how to become a supernatural disciple of Jesus. Core elements of Christian theology are beautifully simplified and secrets of the kingdom of God are revealed in an innovative mix of solid foundational principles coupled with practical application. If you want to step more into your heavenly calling, destiny and purpose and see it manifest on earth, then this guide is for you. Gene and Lauren are the real deal, their lives are a genuine display of people who have been with Jesus. Join them in this book and embark on an exciting journey of an amazing lifestyle with Jesus.

Dr. Mark Birch-Machin,
Founder and Director of Speakers of Life, a Global Prophetic Network
On the Council of the British Isles Council of Prophets
International PhD Scientist and Serial Entrepreneur
Author of "Go Dream" and "Speakers of Life"

Learning
to
Follow Jesus

A Guide for All Believers

Gene and Lauren Lloyd

Published in the United States by
WNM Publishing
www.nomorewounds.org
ministry@nomorewounds.org
facebook.com/woundednomore
@woundednomoredc

Cover design by Meranna

E-book is available under the same title on the Amazon Kindle
platform

Printed in the Unites States of America
ALL RIGHTS RESERVED
First Printing: February 2023

Library of Congress Cataloging-in-Publication Data
Lloyd, Gene and Lauren.
Learning to Follow Jesus / Gene and Lauren Lloyd.
ISBN: 979-8-218-08247-5

Dedicated to everyone who is pursuing the one who speaks the words of eternal life.

"Lord, to whom shall we go? You have the words of eternal life." – John 6:68

Contents

Foreword

Gene and Lauren Lloyd are an amazing couple. I have known them for many years and have spoken with them about what they are doing in the greater Washington, D.C. area. To know them is to know authentic Christians who bring good news to the poor, evangelize the lost, feed the hungry, shelter the homeless, and set into community those who are lonely. They are true followers of Jesus who love to worship God, who live lives filled with awe and wonder regarding the goodness of God and how great is His plan of salvation. Their book, *Learning to Follow Jesus,* is an exciting discipleship manual with twenty-seven short chapters, an introduction and an additional chapter on impartation. It would make a great devotional that could be read in a month. That is if you could stop reading after one chapter. It is written with a sense of joy.

There are three primary basic goals for their book: 1. helping you develop a lifestyle of deep intimacy with God, 2. discovering your true identity and purpose, 3. being equipped to immediately start partnering with God. These goals are facilitated by the disciple learning about the gifts of the Holy

Spirit and the ways of God, by learning who you are in Christ and who Christ is in you, and by learning His word – the Bible. A strong secondary purpose is to enable the believer to learn foundational Christian beliefs. This is a great book especially for new believers – a primer on discipleship – but it is also a great book for all who never really had someone to disciple them. As a result, so many who have been Christians for years weren't taught how to be a victorious disciple of Jesus Christ.

They believe, "Every follower of Jesus needs a solid foundation from the beginning of their faith journey to be effective in their calling. Without it, you are likely to miss out on the greatest opportunity of your life to join the fight of displacing darkness with the light of Jesus. Learning to Follow Jesus puts you in the fight!" This book is for anyone who wants to become a more effective partner co-laboring with Jesus and bringing glory to God by their well-lived lives. A life full of heavenly surprises when the Kingdom of God breaks into our normal routines of life and we, as a result, experience the power of God, the wisdom of God, and the beauty of God. We learn how to allow God's grace to flow through our lives. We are excited to see God add his *super* to our *natural.*

They added short videos of encouragement at the end of each chapter which can be viewed simply by clicking the QR code with your phone.

There is so much great teaching in this book. I hope the new believers from the sacramental denominations will also see Gene and Lauren's hearts that believe there can be empowering grace to strengthen those who receive baptism and who receive communion. Those from other Christian traditions will be blessed if they embrace the practical aspects of *Learning to Follow Jesus.* Gene and Lauren have given us a wonderful discipleship tool.

Randy Clark

D.D., D.Min., Th.D., M.Div., B.S. Religious Studies
Overseer of the apostolic network of Global Awakening
President of Global Awakening Theological Seminary

Foreword

My journey with Jesus began when I asked Jesus into my heart at eight years old. I gave as much of myself as I understood to as much of God as I understood at that time. I had no idea of the adventure this one decision would have in my life. What I know now is that saying "yes" to Jesus literally changes everything. All the great teachers and philosophers said, "Follow my teachings." Jesus simply said, "Follow me." I accepted this invitation of a lifetime and I know no other decision would have transformed me, my life and those I influence more than this one. The same is true for you. People around me modeled following Jesus and many taught me what following Jesus would look like in my life. I have learned to depend on God, trust in Jesus and allow Holy Spirit to be my guide. Spending time with Jesus and studying God's word has been the most important practices as I have been on the journey. I am deeply grateful for those who have poured into my life and the books that continue to help me go deeper in the most important relationship in my life.

The book you have in your hands is an invitation to a roadmap of the life I have enjoyed for well over fifty years. Learning to Follow Jesus provides a path that literally reveals your next step on the journey. Gene and Lauren Lloyd are qualified to write Learning to Follow Jesus because they are following Jesus step by step. Obviously, the Bible can teach you all you need to know about the path to follow Jesus, but Gene and Lauren have taken a marker to highlight the answers, so they are easier to grasp. This book begins with basics - "Who is Jesus" and "Who are you" and takes you into intimacy with God, Jesus and Holy Spirit with practical steps and applications along the way.

I remember the first time I met Gene and Lauren Lloyd. I thought, "God is at work through this couple." Watching their lives over the past years, I can affirm my first thought was true. God is at work in and through them whether it is on a street corner in the worst part of a city or teaching in a beautiful setting. Their desire to disciple others is now a gift to you as they have poured their experience and knowledge in the pages of this book. Don't miss reading every word and enjoying the videos at the end of each chapter!

Blessings on your journey,

Phyllis Hendry Halverson
President Emeritus, Lead Like Jesus

Introduction

Following Jesus is the most incredible journey any human can ever embark upon. We have been invited into the most intriguing, rewarding, exciting, and sometimes confusing, relationship that exists in the universe. God, the creator of the universe, has invited us to partner with Him in transplanting the principles and realities of His kingdom on earth, so that earth mirrors heaven. This has been God's plan for thousands of years—since the beginning of time! It is a partnership birthed from relationship, and the only way we can effectively partner with Him is to dive 100% into this relationship. EVERYTHING in the kingdom of God is birthed from a place of relationship.

This discipleship training course has been developed to provide you with the knowledge and understanding that you need to immediately be effective in the unique calling that God has for your life. The very second you gave your life to Jesus, something inside of you changed. Your identity changed. Your authority changed. God began to speak and declare things into your life that He had prepared just for you since the beginning of time. You have probably wondered at different points in your life about your purpose, the reason you exist, or what you were created to accomplish during your life. We have great news for you! You have a divine purpose thought up in the mind of God long before the world ever existed. Choosing to follow Jesus is the avenue by which you are able to accomplish the mission of your life—it is actually impossible to accomplish without Him! Choosing to follow Him is the only way you can succeed in fulfilling your purpose and destiny.

Maybe you are new to the idea of following Jesus, maybe you spent time in church when you were younger but never really chose to be in a relationship with Him, or maybe you have been a Christian for most of your life, but you realize you are not actually equipped to fulfill the purpose, mission, and destiny God specifically designed for you. Regardless of whether you are new to this journey, or a long-time follower of Jesus, this course will provide you with the foundational principles you need, so that you can live your life with the power and authority Jesus has provided for you. And most importantly, you will receive practical advice on how to immediately apply what you are learning. This is not about learning deep theology; it is about equipping you in a practical way so that you can be powerfully used by God to transform the world around you. Studying deep theological principles will come later in your journey.

We define a disciple as one who accepts and assists in spreading the doctrines of another. The doctrines followers of Jesus are called to accept and spread, are the principles of the kingdom of God. Discipleship training is the process of teaching you, the follower of Jesus, about those principles. To be successful in this course, you simply need to put the concepts into practice. Do not rush through the material. Take time to absorb and apply it to your everyday life. When you are finished, you will find that you have the ability to hear God's voice clearly, you will understand how to represent the fullness of Jesus on the earth, you will know how to partner with Him to release supernatural miracles into people's lives, and you will be greatly accelerated into the rest of your journey.

Each lesson in this course is designed to teach you about what the life of a follower of Jesus should look like so that you can fulfill your God-given purpose and destiny. God had a plan for your life long before you were ever born. You have a vital role to play in the expansion of His kingdom on the earth. That may sound like a big impossible goal to you right now, but that is only because you have not yet learned about who you really are, and how much God wants to partner with you. Each lesson includes practical guidance about a particular topic along with a foundation from the Bible and how to immediately and practically apply what you have learned to your life.

Maybe you have never read the Bible before, or only have a small amount of familiarity with it. So, what is it exactly? The Bible is a collection of 66 different books written from approximately 1400 BC to 95 AD. In it, we get the story of how God created the earth, the history of God's relationship with the patriarchs of our faith and the nation of Israel, prophecies about the future (many of which have already come true), the coming of Jesus, the birth of the Christian faith, stories about the lives of early followers of Jesus, and so many promises from God. It is full of teachings and wisdom that we can use to live our lives in a way that is pleasing to God and to guide us in our mission to make the earth look like heaven.

Each one of the 66 books are further divided into chapters and verses to make it easy to reference different sections. They were not originally written with chapter and verse numbers, but this methodology helps us to study and memorize in a more organized way. Keep this in mind as you read and be sure to read the surrounding chapters and verses to get the full meaning of what is being conveyed. But the Bible is more than just books and stories. It is the written word of God. Each portion of the Bible was written by humans under the inspiration of God. In the book of 2nd Timothy, we are shown how important Scripture is to our lives:

> 2 Timothy 3:17 - "All Scripture is God-breathed and is useful for teaching, rebuking, correcting and training in righteousness, so that the servant of God may be thoroughly equipped for every good work."

You will learn more about how to study the Bible in lesson three, this is just an introduction, so you do not feel lost in the first few lessons. As you go through each lesson, read each referenced Scripture in your Bible, fill in the blanks, and ponder the meaning of each verse. There are many different translations of the Bible; we are using the New International Version in this training course, but you are encouraged to also look up the verses in other translations to get a deeper meaning of each verse. If you do not have a physical Bible, you can use the biblegateway.com website or download one of the many Bible smartphone apps to access many different versions of the Bible for free.

We have also included videos at the end of each lesson where we answer some of the most common questions each topic generates. This is a chance for you to go a little deeper into each subject as we unpack the truth of the gospel. May we be like the Apostle Peter, one of Jesus' original disciples who recognized that Jesus has the words of eternal life. There is nowhere else we can go to receive what He has to offer. So, what are you waiting for? Dive right in!

Lesson One

Who is Jesus?

It is important at the outset of this course to establish a solid foundation for you to learn about the fullness of who Jesus is, all that He encompasses, and everything He represents. We cannot properly represent Him if we do not know what He stands for, what He has accomplished, and what He plans to do in the future. Part of the joy of the journey in our relationship with Jesus is to discover for ourselves the many facets of who He is. He desires to reveal Himself to each of us as our relationship with Him grows. But we also need to build a solid foundation so that as we continue in this relationship, we do not become deceived by any teaching that misrepresents Jesus or defines Him as someone He is not. The best way for any believer to learn about Jesus is to study the Bible and let the reality of who He is soak into our heart, mind, and spirit. Get your Bible ready, we have a lot of reading to do this week.

Jesus is the most incredible person you will ever meet. But He is more than a person. He is God. He left heaven to be born on earth and live as a man for a very specific purpose. And once that purpose was completed, He returned to heaven. The idea that Jesus is God can be confusing to new believers as well as those who have been attending church for many years, so let us clear up that confusion with some definitions. There is one God who eternally exists as three distinct persons. This is often referred to as the Godhead or the Trinity. These three distinct persons are the Father, Son (Jesus), and Holy Spirit. It is important to note here that this is not simply three different ways God represents Himself to humanity. We will discuss the Trinity more in-depth in lesson five, but for now, know that the Bible defines Jesus as God in various places. Here is one of them:

> *Titus 2:13 - "while we wait for the blessed hope—the appearing of the glory of our great _____ and Savior, _____ ..."*

What else does the Bible teach us about Jesus? A lot. It is important for you to view Jesus, not only from the perspective of His short life on earth, but from the greater perspective of all that He encompasses. Many followers of Jesus do not recognize the fullness of who He is because they do not undertake the time to study what the Bible reveals about Him. If you submit your life to someone, it is a good idea to know everything about them that you can. You wouldn't just take people's word for it, would you? You would want to learn everything about the person you are choosing to follow. The first chapter of John teaches us some key pieces about Jesus:

Jesus existed before all of time.

> *John 1:1-2 – "_____ was the Word, and the Word was with God, and the Word was God. He was _____ God in the beginning."*

Jesus is the creator of all things.

*John 1:3 – "Through him _____ were made;
without him nothing was made that has been made."*

Jesus gives us the right to become the children of God.

*John 1:12 – "to those who believed in his name, he gave
the _____ to become children of God..."*

He came to earth to reveal Himself as the Messiah of the Jewish faith and to offer Himself as the ultimate sacrifice for the sins of all humans who ever have or ever will exist. The Messiah was the one who was coming to save Israel and the rest of the world. We will discuss some of the background to this in more detail in lesson nine when we discuss the history of people following God throughout different generations. But for now, you need to know that the primary reason Jesus came to earth was to provide a perfect sacrifice for the sins of all humanity. It is this sacrifice that opens the door for us to have eternal life and communion with God. Jesus is the only way to the Father and the only way to eternal life. There is no other way but through Him.

*John 3:16 – "For God so loved the world that he
_____ his one and only Son, that whoever believes
in him shall not perish but have _____."*

*Hebrews 10:12- "But when this priest (Jesus) had offered
_____ _____ one sacrifice for _____, he sat
down at the right hand of God."*

*John 14:6 – "Jesus answered, 'I am the _____ and
the _____ and the _____. _____ comes
to the Father except through _____.'"*

Jesus was supernaturally born by a virgin named Mary, lived on the earth as a human for about 33 years, and during the final few years of His physical life, He taught about the kingdom of God and performed many miracles. He later told His disciples that they would do what He did and greater things. This was not just a promise for the few men He was talking to that day. This was a promise for every person who ever chooses to follow Him. You can do what Jesus did!

> *John 14:12 – "Very truly I tell you, whoever believes in me will do the _____ I have been doing, and they will do even _____ things than these..."*

The story of Jesus starts long before He was born on earth. Prophets foretold His coming for thousands of years and longed for the day when their Messiah would come. He came onto the scene in the midst of the Roman empire's rule in Jerusalem and the surrounding regions. But He did not come in the way many Jews expected. They were expecting a conquering king who would restore the nation of Israel and overthrow their conquerors. Jesus' mission was so much bigger than one nation during one time in history. He had come to save the entire world.

His teachings challenged the religious leaders of that day who enforced rules and regulations on the Jewish people but did not have an understanding of the love of God. They were not happy with this "new guy" who was teaching with an authority and power they had never seen before. They did not like the idea of an outsider healing people's sicknesses and were jealous of the large crowds of people gathered to hear His teachings. So, they conspired to have Him killed and convinced the local Roman authority to crucify Him on a cross. What they did not know was that this was all part of His original plan.

Jesus went to the cross willingly to provide forgiveness your sins and all the sins of the world, but to get a better picture of what that encompassed, go to your Bible and read the story of the crucifixion of Jesus found in Luke 22:1 – Luke 23:55, then answer these questions:

Who betrayed Jesus?

_____

Who came to arrest Jesus?

_____

How did Jesus respond to His arrest?

_____

Who was crucified alongside Jesus?

_____

There is a key piece to this story that cannot be left out. If it is, we lose a big part of what Jesus accomplished. He did not stay in the grave! Go back to your Bible and continue the story by reading all of Luke chapter 24. The death of Jesus paid for the sins of all humanity for all time. The resurrection of Jesus shows His power over death and gives us the assurance that when our physical bodies die, we will be resurrected at some point and live forever with Him. Because of His sacrifice, and our acceptance of Him as our savior, we have been transformed into something new. You may still look the same physically, but an amazing change took place when you gave your life to Jesus.

Before Jesus left the earth, He promised that He would return one day for all those who follow Him. We do not know when that will occur. It may be in your lifetime, and it may be hundreds of years from now, but we do know it will happen because He always keeps His promises. When that day comes, every person from all of time and history who chose to follow God will spend eternity with Him.

John 14:3 – "if I go and prepare a place for you, I will _____ and take you to be with me that you also may be where I am."

1 Corinthians 5:8 – "We are confident, I say, and would prefer to be away from the _____ and at _____ with the Lord."

And there is still so much more to who He is! A few pages in a book can never do it justice. Jesus is God, He is our Savior, He is our King, He is our best friend, and so much more. As you continue this journey with the Lord you will learn about His many attributes, and He will reveal Himself to you in many unique ways. You will discover that He is exactly what you need when you need it. Ask Him who He is for you today. As you do this, you will recognize Him speaking to you and sharing with you those attributes of Himself every day. This lesson just barely scratches the surface. Dig deep as you continue to study, and you will experience for yourself how amazing He is and how much more He wants to reveal to you.

Video Wrap Up – Scan the QR code below to hear some final thoughts from Gene and Lauren about a common question on this topic:

Lesson Two

Who Are You?

It seems as if there are so many books, programs, and movements that are trying to tell us who we should be or who we should become. Society tries to define us by numbers, letter combinations, race, gender, political beliefs, or our personalities. God, the one who created us, knows us better than we know ourselves and yet we seldom go to Him to define who we are. The true identity of a follower of Jesus must be understood in order to fulfill your life's purpose and mission. If you do not know who you are, you will never be able to fully understand how much God loves you, the purpose for which you were created, and the authority that you carry. One of the greatest problems we have in Christianity today is that followers of Jesus do not know who they really are, and this is a central reason as to why the church has not been as effective in changing culture. When you know who you are, and you know the mission you have been given by your King, changing culture becomes a lot easier. How much impact could we have if we really believed what Jesus said about us? What would our communities, cities, and nations look like if we lived from the perspective of our true identity? So, who does Jesus say that you are?

> *Matthew 5:13-14 – "You are the _____ of the earth. But if the salt loses its saltiness, how can it be made salty again? It is no longer good for _____, except to be thrown out and trampled underfoot. You are the _____ of the world. A town built on a hill cannot be _____."*

If we are the light of the world, darkness should flee when we show up. When you turn a light on in a room, the darkness does not get to choose if it wants to stay in that room. It does not have a choice. The light forces it from the room. This should be the same reaction when a follower of Jesus encounters any spiritual darkness. Darkness should run as soon as you show up. This is part of your identity.

> *2 Corinthians 5:20 – "We are therefore Christ's _____, as though God were making his appeal through us..."*

> *John 20:21 – "Peace be with you! As the Father has _____ me, I am _____ you."*

> *John 14:13-14 – "And I will do _____ you ask in my name, so that the Father may be glorified in the Son. You may ask me for _____ in my name, and I will do it."*

If we are His ambassadors, sent to continue the same purpose He was sent for, we get to represent the fullness of who He is and what He represents. Ambassadors speak on behalf of the one who sent them. If you are an ambassador for the United States, and you promise aid to a nation, they know your promise is backed up by the financial stability of the United States. And if you threaten war, they know your threat is backed up by a powerful military force. If a small island nation threatened war against someone, it would not be a strong threat, because it would be unlikely that they could do any real harm. The words that an ambassador speaks carry the weight of the nation that they represent. In our case, as ambassadors for Jesus, our words carry the weight of the kingdom of Heaven; the most powerful kingdom in all of existence. This is part of your new identity in Christ.

> *Ephesians 2:6-7 – "And God _____ us up with Christ and _____ us with him in the heavenly realms in Christ Jesus, in order that in the coming ages he might show the incomparable riches of his grace, expressed in his kindness to us in Christ Jesus."*

If we are seated with Christ, we need to live with the level of authority that position gives us. Some authority is available to all followers of Jesus, such as the authority to heal sickness or decree the will of God that we will discuss in later lessons. But specific authority is given to individual followers of Jesus within the area we have been assigned. Where we are assigned is an important piece of this discussion. An ambassador to Ethiopia does not have any authority in Germany. An ambassador to Ethiopia cannot make promises to the leaders of Germany because there is no authority backing up their words. Our specific authority as followers of Jesus is tied to the assignment, or the calling, that is on our lives. These assignments can be different in different seasons of our lives, and part of your journey with Jesus is to discover the assignment He has for you right now, and where He is leading you next. We can ask Him what our assignment is and how we do it. He has all the answers. As you grow in faith and continue on this journey you will learn more about how to operate in the fullness of the authority that you have been given. This is also part of your new identity in Christ.

John 14:12 – "Very truly I tell you, whoever believes in me will do the _____ I have been doing, and they will do even _____ things than these..."

Jesus said that we would do greater things than He did. Think about that for a minute. Think about some of the miracles recorded in the Bible. Healing the sick, raising the dead, calming storms, and walking on water are all things that Jesus did. And he said we would do greater things. Greater things! This gives God greater glory and shows people the power of who He is through us. It leads people to Him, not us. The great news here is that God wants to partner with us. Everyone who chooses to follow Jesus is invited into an opportunity to partner with Him. This is because Jesus wants the earth to look like heaven and He even taught us to pray from that perspective:

Matthew 6:9-10 – "This, then, is how you should pray: Our Father in heaven, hallowed be your name, your kingdom come, your will be done, on _____ as it is in _____ ."'

What would change on earth if it suddenly looked like heaven? There is no sickness or disease in heaven. There is no hatred in heaven. There is no crime in heaven. There is no racism in heaven. And the list goes on. Anything that does not exist in heaven is not part of God's kingdom. We want the earth to look like heaven. We accomplish this by representing Jesus and the principles of His kingdom everywhere we go. Think about what it looks like to represent Jesus. Think about the reality of what that means for you, about the impact you can have when you partner with Him to accomplish His mission on the earth. Pause and take a few minutes to write down a few thoughts on what you think your world would look like if you partnered with Jesus in every part of your life.

_____

_____

_____

_____

_____

_____

Followers of Jesus need to view everything through the lens of the perspective of the Kingdom of God. You must consider what is happening in His kingdom, what His goal is for a situation, and what He wants to occur on the earth. That is thinking from a kingdom perspective. Any idea born through the world's perspective can never compete with what is born through a kingdom perspective. Political positions, popular culture, and the idea of society progressing to accept things that were once considered reprehensible are all flavored with the perspective of the world. We do not need the world's perspective. Our position with Jesus provides us with a kingdom perspective that, when we tap into it, gives us a greater degree of wisdom and knowledge about any topic or situation.

It is a big mission, with a lot of moving pieces, and you have a vital role to play. You were uniquely created with a specific purpose to help fulfill God's plan to establish His kingdom principles on the earth. Do not let any person, thought, or perspective ever sway you from this reality. God wants to partner with you more than you want to partner with Him. He has been thinking about you since before the world was ever created!

Read Mark 16:17-18 then answer this question:

Who is this promise for?

_____

Read John 20:21 and answer this question:

How have you been sent?

_____

This was not just for the disciples; it is for every believer! Jesus prayed in John 17:20-21 that, through all of us, the world would believe He was sent by the Father. Many of the people used powerfully by God in the early church were not part of Jesus' original 12 disciples. They were people who believed as a result of the teaching of the disciples. Some even believed as a result of supernatural encounters with God that happened after Jesus left the earth. And God used these people to heal the sick, raise the dead, cast out demons, and release the message of the gospel of Jesus. This mission and lifestyle is for every follower of Jesus!

Read John 15:15 and answer this question:

How does Jesus refer to you?

_____

Read John 15:1-8

Do you see the way God designed our relationship with Him to intertwine in a very intimate way? Everything we do as believers need to come from this place of intimate relationship with Jesus, the Holy Spirit, and the Father. Anything else risks becoming an unhealthy perspective. Our lives, our service, our ministry, and the way we view and treat others all need to flow from this place of intimacy.

Read John 15:5 again and answer this question:

What can you do without Jesus?

_____

That is right, absolutely nothing!

This is who you have been transformed into as a result of what Jesus did for you! It has nothing to do with what you have done. You can never earn salvation and you can never earn this new identity. It is a gift from God! How is this possible? How is it that someone can suddenly become a new person? It is possible because the supernatural power of God causes a transformation to take place within you the very second you say yes to Jesus.

Galatians 2:20 starts with this statement: *"I have been crucified with Christ."* Some translations say co-crucified, which is an even better way to describe what happened. How is that possible if He was crucified thousands of years before you were born? In the spiritual realm, when He was crucified, you were hanging on the cross with Him. All of humanity was hanging on the cross with Him. The nail that pierced His hands pierced yours as well. It may be difficult to imagine but it is the spiritual reality of what occurred.

The verse continues with this: *"and I no longer live, but Christ lives in me."* You died. Your old life ended the very second that you said yes to Jesus and you were brought into a new life. The life we now live is from Christ, and for Christ, with Christ in us! You are a new creation! Not because of anything that you accomplished, but because of what Jesus accomplished. Nothing and no one can ever cancel out His accomplishment or take away your right to be called a son or daughter of God. Consider this, you were physically born as a result of the actions of your parents. You are not their son or daughter because of anything you did. There is nothing you can ever do to stop being their son or daughter. It is a fact, it is a reality, and nothing can change it. Your new identity in Christ is very similar. It is by His actions alone that we can have this new identity.

As you continue on this journey with Jesus, He will reveal to you more about who you are, your purpose and destiny on the earth, how He wants to use you to help make the world look like His kingdom, and the specific role He wants you to play in impacting other people's lives. The more time you spend with Jesus, the more you will realize that this exciting lifelong journey is the best way to live!

Video Wrap Up – Scan the QR code below to hear some final thoughts from Gene and Lauren about a common question on this topic:

Lesson Three

How to Study the Bible

Every follower of Jesus should take time every day to read and study the Bible. Remember from the introduction at the beginning of this course that 2 Timothy 3:17 says:

> *"All Scripture is God-breathed and is useful for teaching, rebuking, correcting and training in righteousness, so that the servant of God may be thoroughly equipped for every good work."*

What this essentially means is that the Bible is the written word of God, and that God inspired people to write down His words so that we would all have a solid foundation for living a life dedicated to His purpose. The Bible is full of content that teaches us how to live our lives in relationship with each other and God. Some stories give us great examples of things we should not do. Some show us historical accounts of what happened when the people of God were obedient and what happened when they were disobedient. The Bible is full of instruction, revelation, and insight into the ways of God. It is also the greatest love story that has ever been written!

We have found a simple idea to be true. If you want God to speak to you, you should start by studying His written word. When we show that we care about what He has already spoken, He often begins to speak to us directly. Reading and studying the Bible should be thought of as more than just a requirement of the Christian lifestyle, it should be thought of as an exciting journey into the mind of God to learn about who He is and to grow deeper in our relationship with Him. In fact, reading the Bible is not about gaining book knowledge; the goal is to know the author. Most books are read to understand the content. But when you read a biography, you read to know about the person who is the subject of the book. When we read the Bible, our primary aim is to know HIM better. So, what is the best way to study the Bible? Well, there are a lot of different ideas and approaches to this topic and no single approach is necessarily the best. But there are a few common ideas that we can use as guidelines to help us study what God has spoken in a healthy way so that we do not end up with a skewed perspective about what He is speaking.

Prayer

It is always best to start with prayer. Always take time to pray before you read the Bible, and specifically ask God to make His written word come alive to you as you read it. Our primary goal when reading the Bible is to get to know Him. Our primary goal is not knowledge, it is to know our God. So, ask God to draw you deeper into a relationship with Him while you read.

Context

It is often said that context is the key to properly interpreting something. It is dangerous to lift one verse out of the Bible and build a set of beliefs from that one single verse.

This has happened many times in history, and it usually takes people down a path of believing something about God that is not true. The way we avoid this pitfall is to study the context of what God has said by applying a few simple techniques:

- **First,** when reading a specific verse, always read it as part of the complete chapter or with the surrounding verses to gain a more complete understanding of what it means. Even better, read it as part of the entire book to see where it fits in the full narrative.
- **Second,** look for words, phrases, or ideas that repeat so you can see how the verse relates to other verses within the chapter.
- **Third,** pay attention to the facts about people, places, or events mentioned in the verse or chapter.
- **Fourth,** consider the cultural context of when the content was written, who the original audience was, and what it may have meant in that particular era of time.

Keep in mind that the meaning of the Bible never changes. The proper interpretation is to discover what the author's original intent was when it was written. It means today exactly what it meant when it was originally penned, and it conveys exactly what God wants it to convey. Our understanding of what it is saying and the revelation that God gives to us about a particular passage may grow over time, but the meaning never changes. The more we read and study His written word, the more we learn about Him, about His perspectives, and about how we can apply those perspectives to our lives.

Dig Deeper

God will also speak to you specifically through the Bible. As you read, ask Him to speak into the situations of your life through the verses you are reading. Ask Him to reveal another aspect of His nature. Ask Him to give you wisdom about the

topic you are studying. He is so good at revealing a truth we
need to hear right now from something that was written
thousands of years ago. He is infinitely wise and able to cause
the Scripture to come alive to us and give us a deeper meaning.
Ask Him questions! Ask Him about what you are reading, about
the situation(s) the Holy Spirit inspired the writer to speak into,
and listen closely for His answers.

Re-read

Reading the same book multiple times gives you a greater
familiarity with what it covers. If you have watched the same
movie many different times, you tend to know when a particular
scene is coming up, have memorized some of the lines, and
know how the movie flows from beginning to end. We should
have an even greater level of knowledge of the Bible, and that
comes when we read and re-read the different books or sections
many times.

Different Bible Translations

As mentioned in the introduction, there are many
different Bible translations. It is highly beneficial to read the
Bible in different translations to get a deeper meaning of what
God is speaking. One solution would be to learn the ancient
Hebrew and Greek languages, but that is not the easiest thing to
do, and not always practical, so the alternative is to read how
different experts have translated the text over the years. It can
be confusing when you start to look at all the available
translations that exist, but as you dive into reading from these
different translations, you will see the value for yourself. We
have included a chart from biblegateway.com that provides an
overview of where different translations fall on a spectrum from
word-for-word to thought-for-thought. We encourage you to
use the biblegateway.com website to become familiar with
different versions of the Bible as you continue to study.

BIBLE TRANSLATIONS

The Bible was originally written in:
HEBREW, ARAMAIC, and GREEK.

Freely read the Bible on Bible Gateway in more than 200 versions and more than 70 languages including:

TWO APPROACHES
Two main philosophies behind translating the Bible range on a continuum between:

▶ **WORD-FOR-WORD**
Adhering to the words and structure of the original language without sacrificing clarity.

▶ **THOUGHT-FOR-THOUGHT**
Prioritizing clarity and understanding of the meaning of the original language without sacrificing accuracy.

Amplified Bible	The Message
Christian Standard Bible	Modern English Version
Common English Bible	New American Bible (Revised Edition)
Contemporary English Version	New American Standard Bible
Easy-to-Read Version	New Century Version
Evangelical Heritage Version	New English Translation
English Standard Version	New International Reader's Version
God's Word	New International Version
Good News Translation	New King James Version
International Children's Bible	New Living Translation
International Standard Version	New Revised Standard Version
King James Version	Revised Standard Version
The Living Bible	The Voice

Bible translations represented in this spectrum by their abbreviations are available for reading on Bible Gateway

WORD-FOR-WORD .... THOUGHT-FOR-THOUGHT

NASB | ESV RSV | NKJV | | NRSV | NET | GW ISV | CEB | GNT ERV | LIVING
AMP | KJV MEV CSB EHV NABRE | NIV | NCV/ICB NLT NIrV | CEV | MSG
INTERLINEAR | | VOICE

External Sources

As you become more familiar with the Bible, and after you have read it through multiple times, you should begin to look at other external sources to help you study. These sources will help you go even deeper into the meanings of words within the context and historical setting of how they were used when the Bible was written as well as the thoughts of theologians.

- Bible concordances – provide an index of words in the Bible in alphabetical order, sometimes with the original Hebrew or Greek words included.
- Bible dictionaries – these are similar to a normal dictionary, but with a focus on words found in the Bible.
- Bible commentaries – explanations and interpretations written by theologians to expound on different portions of the Bible.

Each of the methods outlined in this lesson will help you go deeper with God. Start with just your Bible and ask Holy Spirit to reveal the truth of His word to you. Do not consult external sources right away, let some time pass to grow on your own with Holy Spirit so a solid foundation can be built. Discuss revelations and questions with a trusted pastor or spiritual adviser who can make sure you are heading in the right direction. You can add the thoughts of others into the mix later, but it is best to grow in your own ability to hear the Lord for yourself before you dig into the commentaries and dictionaries. As you start to add in external sources, get your spiritual leaders' advice on what you should be reading. Many authors have written many different books on biblical subjects, and they are not all in agreement. It is best to avoid incorrect theology in the beginning so that you will recognize it more easily as you continue to grow in your faith. Learning about God and getting to know Him is a lifelong journey, and one we will all continue likely even throughout eternity, so enjoy the journey!

Video Wrap Up – Scan the QR code below to hear some final thoughts from Gene and Lauren about a common question on this topic:

Lesson Four

Purpose of the Christian Life

So, you have given your life to Jesus, but what does that really mean? What does it mean to follow Jesus, to be a Christian, and what is your life supposed to look like now that you made this major life-changing decision? As you learned in lesson two, following Jesus changes your identity into someone who represents Jesus on the earth. The simple answer to this opening question is that every follower of Jesus should continue the work Jesus started a few thousand years ago. In John 20:21, Jesus said, "As the Father has sent me, I am sending you." This is such a powerful statement that defines the core purpose of every follower of Jesus. We like to frame it like this: your mission is to make disciples and teach them how to make disciples. But before you can start doing that, you need to have a solid foundation of what it means to be a disciple of Jesus, which requires a deeper understanding of why Jesus came to earth.

John 20:21 starts with, *"As the Father sent me,"* so we should ask, how was Jesus sent? What was the purpose the

Father had for Jesus? Of course, we know that Jesus came into the world for the purpose of providing salvation to all of humanity. But He was also sent to spread the good news of the kingdom of God. He was sent to share with all of us what God's kingdom is like, what it represents, how it operates, and to tell us that His kingdom will exist for all of eternity. He is the King of all kings. He is reigning now and will continue to reign for all of eternity as King over everything. Sharing the reality of the kingdom was a major part of His mission and it is a major part of our mission as well.

> Luke 4:42 - *"I must proclaim the _____ of the kingdom of God to the other towns also, because that is why I was _____."*

We continue the work of Jesus by spreading the good news of the kingdom of God. As a follower of Jesus, you have an opportunity to change the world. As you learn more about Jesus, by sitting at His feet, and by reading His word, you can apply that knowledge to your life, and share it with others. It is a lifelong journey of getting to know more about Him and sharing the reality of who He is with others. We change the world by making disciples. We change the world by showing the world who Jesus is. Every person who accepts Jesus as their savior is one more person shifting their focus away from the world and onto the things of God's kingdom! Jesus gave us the correct focus when He gave us this model prayer:

> Matt 6:9-13 – *"This, then, is how you should pray: Our Father in heaven, hallowed be your name, your _____ come, your _____ be done, on _____ as it is in _____. Give us today our daily bread. And forgive us our debts, as we also have forgiven our debtors. And lead us not into temptation, but deliver us from the evil one."*

We need to make the earth look like heaven. We need to take the ideas and principles of God's kingdom and spread them around the earth so that all people will shed the perspectives and ideas of the world and replace them with the ones from His kingdom. When people realize who God is, what He stands for, how much He loves them, and what His plans are for their lives, they will surrender everything to Him. Apart from that revelation, people just see following Jesus as a religious belief, or a set of rules that need to be followed. Sometimes they see this way of life as an archaic way of thinking. But when people have the revelation of who God is, it changes the way they view everything. That is where you are now. You decided to follow Jesus, and you are on the journey to discovering more about Him, and more about His plan for your life.

Every person in all of creation has an individual purpose that adds to the overall purpose of expanding God's kingdom. Some refer to this as our life's calling, others call it the reason for living. Whatever way you frame it, it basically means the same thing. We have been created with a divinely given purpose and a divinely given identity to impact the people in our spheres of influence. There are people you can impact that others can never impact. There are places you will go that others will never go. Do not discount your value to the kingdom of God! Your past is irrelevant to the fulfillment of your future.

You can start right now! Ask God to show you the things in your life that are based on the principles of the world. Write down what He tells you here:

_____
_____
_____
_____
_____
_____

Now, ask Him to show you His kingdom principles that He wants to give you in exchange for the worldly ones. Write those down here:

_____

_____

_____

_____

_____

_____

Each principle that God reveals to you is an invitation to go deeper in your relationship with Him. He longs for you to be fully transformed into the person He created you to be. As you learn more about His kingdom, you will begin to recognize the differences between His kingdom and the kingdom of darkness that covers this world. It will be like night and day. One of the biggest challenges in learning what following Jesus looks like practically in everyday life, is learning about His perspective on all things. The reason why this is so challenging is that we all form our own opinions from what we have learned in school, from family, in church, and through life experiences. We must be willing to accept that some of those opinions are wrong. What makes them wrong is simple; if they are not in agreement with the Bible, they automatically become wrong. This is why knowing His perspective is so important.

Take politics for example. People form political opinions based on a lot of factors, but rarely have a conversation with God about whether or not those opinions line up with His ideas. Once we settle into our political party preferences, we tend to stay there for a very long time unless something dislodges us from that way of thinking. This is true in other areas of our lives as well, but the topic of politics is one that everyone can easily associate with a rigid posture. Jesus is not part of any political party. He is an everlasting King ruling an everlasting kingdom. His kingdom perspectives need to be our number one priority. We are called to lay aside everything else when we choose to follow Him. We replace our opinions with His, and they are so much better than anything we could ever come up with on our own.

It is very difficult to hear God clearly when we are holding tightly onto an idea. Our own desires and motives can keep us from knowing what actions to take in our lives. Maybe you like the idea of working for a particular company so much that you are constantly praying for an opening in that company without asking God if working there is part of His plan for you. The better method would be to ask God if it is the place where He wants you. The examples here are endless. We need to learn to view everything in life through the lens of the perspective of His kingdom. It takes time to develop this skill, but the quicker you figure it out, it will lessen the chance of you taking a turn down the wrong path for your specific life mission.

We have many examples in the Bible of people choosing to live from a kingdom perspective, even when it made no sense. Abraham left the safety and security of His family in simple obedience, not knowing where God would lead him:

> *Genesis 12:1-4 - "The Lord had said to Abram, Go from your country, your people and your father's household to the land I will _____ you...so Abram _____, as the Lord had _____ him"*

Joseph and Mary – married and gave birth to Jesus based on the words of an angel:

> *Matthew 1:20 - "...an angel of the Lord appeared to him in a dream and said, "Joseph son of David, do not be _____ to take Mary home as your wife..."*

> *Luke 1:38 – "I am the Lord's _____, Mary answered. May your word to me be _____."*

Saul/Paul – shifted his entire life based on one encounter with Jesus:

Acts 9:5-6 - "Who are you, Lord?" Saul asked. "I am Jesus, whom you are persecuting," he replied. "Now get up and _____ into the city, and you will be _____ what you must _____."

And the list goes on, from prophets who spoke things that sounded crazy to followers of Jesus giving up everything to follow their King. Their example should be more than a historical study for us, it should spur us to pursue living our lives from a kingdom perspective. This is the ultimate purpose of living a lifestyle of following Jesus. He leads, we follow, in whatever way that He directs us. Non-believers may think we are crazy, but that is usually a good sign that we are on the right path!

As you grow in your faith and your love for Jesus, you will want to start sharing it with others. His love is infectious and hard to hold inside. It is like wanting to tell everyone about an amazing person you started dating. You do not keep it a secret, you share it with everyone you know. Your relationship with Jesus is something designed to be shared with others so that they can be introduced to Him as well. The expansion of the kingdom of God on earth and the gospel message can be summed up in one simple phrase: make disciples and teach them to make disciples. You get to be part of the process!

Share the testimony of what God has done in your life. People will argue about religion, but they cannot argue with you about your own personal story. Sharing your story can be a great encouragement to others who have had similar experiences because they will be able to relate to what you are sharing and think about how their own life could be different if they experience what you have come to know as truth. Sometimes this story is told simply by the way you live your life. People will recognize that a change has occurred in your life when you start following Jesus. They will wonder why you are no longer doing certain things, and why you are acting differently. The way you live your life is one of the greatest ways to show people what Jesus represents.

Pray for people who are sick or injured. You learned about your identity in lesson two. You know that you represent Jesus. So, pray for people who need a miracle in their life. This is a powerful way to introduce someone to Jesus. Do you know what happens when someone is supernaturally healed? They never forget about it. Every day of not living with the injury or pain is another day they remember what Jesus did for them. This is what it looks like to represent Jesus in everyday life. Live the love of Jesus every day and you will see how easy it is to introduce others to our amazing King.

Video Wrap Up – Scan the QR code below to hear some final thoughts from Gene and Lauren about a common question on this topic:

Lesson Five

The Trinity

Within Christianity, you will often hear God referred to in different ways. Sometimes we just say God, other times we say Father, or Jesus, or Holy Spirit. It can be difficult to understand who God is in His entirety without understanding the reality that He is a triune being. This is referred to as the Trinity, or sometimes the Godhead. The Trinity is best described as three distinct persons in one. But this definition does not clear up the mystery. As you mature in your faith, you will encounter God in many different ways and the doctrine of the Trinity will become clearer, but it is valuable for you to have a foundational understanding now as well as experiential ones as you continue in your faith.

Christianity is monotheistic, meaning a belief in only one God. We serve one God, and only one God. The Jewish faith, which is the foundation for Christianity, has always affirmed that there is one God. It was a unique thing among the different cultures thousands of years ago because most religions of that time served many different false gods, whose origin we will discuss in lesson fourteen. We find this to be true with many religions in today's culture as well. The fact that we serve one God, the one true God, and Him alone is important because Scripture informs us that there is only one God, and we are to serve Him alone:

> *Deuteronomy 4:39 – "Acknowledge and take to heart this day that the Lord is God in heaven above and on the earth below. There is _____ other."*

> *Deuteronomy 6:13-14 – "Fear the Lord your God, serve him _____ and take your oaths in his name. Do not _____ other gods, the gods of the peoples around you;"*

> *1 Timothy 1:17 – "Now to the King eternal, immortal, invisible, the _____ God, be honor and glory forever and ever. Amen."*

He is one God, who by His very nature, exists as three distinct, wholly equal, and inseparable persons: Father, Son, and Holy Spirit. Knowing Him in this way is a deeper and more intimate understanding of His nature. Some have used different analogies to try and explain this difficult concept by showing that an egg is made up of yolk, white, and shell, and yet it is one egg. Or that water can be in the form of a liquid, gas, or solid and yet is still the same molecule. On the surface, these analogies seem to help with understanding the Trinity by showing there are things in nature made up of multiple parts, but these are actually elementary descriptions that verge on a theological perspective known as tritheism, which is a belief that Father, Son, and Holy Spirit are three separate divine beings. It is difficult for our human minds to fully grasp the concept of the Trinity. But be encouraged, theologians have wrestled with this for centuries without being able to perfectly describe this mystery. What we see in the Bible is that, from the very beginning of time, God is referred to in the plurality:

Genesis 1:26 - Then God said, "Let us make mankind in our image, in our likeness, so that they may rule over the fish in the sea and the birds in the sky, over the livestock and all the wild animals, and over all the creatures that move along the ground."

There is very little content in the Old Testament of the Bible that points directly to the Trinity, but there are instances where we can see different representations of the Godhead that show us some of the distinctions. God interacted with humanity in various ways during ancient times. In Genesis 16:7-13, the Angel of God is interacted with and treated as God by Hagar. It is debatable what member of the Trinity this one, but some believe to have been Jesus before His incarnation, which is known as Christophany. Jesus himself said in John 5:46 that Moses wrote about Him, which could be a reference to some of these encounters. Abraham also received a visit from three men in Genesis chapter 18 who are described as God and two angels. Again, we do not know which member of the Trinity spoke with Abraham in this instance, but when we look at the totality of Scripture, some of the pointers become more clear.

The New Testament contains many more definitive pointers to the Trinity that reveal God in three distinct persons. One great example is what occurred immediately after Jesus was baptized. This verse shows us all three members of the Trinity at the same time, and it shows the three distinct persons of the Trinity interacting with each other. There is probably no better place in Scripture where we see these distinctions so clearly:

Mark 1:10-11 – "Just as Jesus was coming up out of the water, he saw heaven being torn open and the _____ descending on him like a dove. And a _____ came from heaven: "You are my _____, whom I love; with you I am well pleased."

Some Scriptures tell us Jesus is God:

> *Hebrews 1:8 – "But about the _____ he says, 'Your throne, O _____, will last for ever and ever; a scepter of justice will be the scepter of your kingdom.'"*

> *Romans 9:5 – "Theirs are the patriarchs, and from them is traced the human ancestry of the _____, who is _____ over all, forever praised!"*

Some Scriptures tell us the Father is God:

> *Romans 1:7 – "...Grace and peace to you from _____ our _____ and from the Lord Jesus Christ."*

> *1 Corinthians 1:3 – "Grace and peace to you from _____ our _____ and the Lord Jesus Christ."*

Some Scriptures tell us Holy Spirit is God:

> *Acts 5:3-4 – "Then Peter said, 'Ananias, how is it that Satan has so filled your heart that you have lied to the _____ and have kept for yourself some of the money you received for the land? Did not it belong to you before it was sold? And after it was sold, was not the money at your disposal? What made you think of doing such a thing? You have not lied just to human beings but to God."*

> *Ephesians 4:30 – "And do not grieve the _____ of _____"*

These different verses show us that there is one God who exists as three different persons, that there is a distinction between each person of the Trinity, and that they are not simply different representations of God. Each person of the Trinity is fully God. Jesus is not 1/3 God. The Father is not 1/3 God. Holy Spirit is not 1/3 God. Each is fully God and fully distinct at the same time. The idea that one God can be three different persons may still be a bit confusing to you, or hard to understand, but as you grow in your relationship with the Father, Jesus, and Holy Spirit it will become clearer. Sometimes experience is the best teacher.

While it may be difficult for us to fully understand in our human minds the concept of the triune nature of God, we need to remember that He is so much greater than we are and that there are many things we will likely not fully understand while we live out our human existence. Some things will only be revealed after our human life on earth comes to an end and we step into eternity with the Lord. It is important to reiterate that each member of the Godhead is fully God, one does not have more power or authority than the other, nor is there any competition between each member of the Trinity. They are equal in every way. Jesus made this declaration after His resurrection regarding His authority:

> *Matthew 28:18 – "All_____in heaven and on earth has been given to me."*

The fact that He has all authority does not mean that the Father and Holy Spirit do not have authority. The Father has all authority, the Son has all authority, and Holy Spirit has all authority. We can pray to any member of the Trinity, and we are praying to the God who has all power and authority. This is a great mystery, and it can take time to digest how this can be so, but like many things in our journey with the Lord, we take it by faith. Take a few minutes to think through and answer the following questions about your understanding of the Trinity.

Who is the Father?

_____

_____

Who is the Son?

_____

_____

_____

Who is Holy Spirit?

_____

_____

_____

What part of the Trinity still confuses you?

_____

_____

_____

_____

Video Wrap Up – Scan the QR code below to hear some final thoughts from Gene and Lauren about a common question on this topic:

Lesson Six

Sitting at the Feet of Jesus

Following Jesus is not just some simple religion. It is a relationship, and like any other relationship, if we want it to grow, we need to be intentional about spending time with Him. In John 15, Jesus gives us an incredible example of our dependence on Him. He says quite simply that we can do nothing without Him. Think about that for a minute and let it soak in. You can do nothing without Jesus. He is the one that created your lungs to breathe. He is the one that causes your heart to beat. He is the one that gives you the power to do anything.

> *John 15:4-5 – "Remain in me, as I also remain in you. No branch can bear fruit by itself; it must remain in the vine. Neither can you bear fruit unless you remain in me. Neither can you bear fruit unless you remain in me. I am the vine; you are the branches. If you remain in me and I in you, you will bear much fruit; apart from me you can do nothing."*

Now consider that God has a divine purpose for your life. You have been uniquely created to fulfill a particular purpose throughout your life, but the only way any of us can be successful in completing every aspect of that purpose is if we fully recognize that we cannot do any of it without Jesus. He is the source of everything that we need. No one can ever fulfill their God-given purpose if they do not fully understand who they are. And the only way we can ever discover the fullness of our identity is to sit at the feet of Jesus. He created us, He knows everything about us, and only He can reveal all the aspects of our identity to us.

In John 10:27, Jesus tells us that His sheep hear His voice. Those who follow Him recognize His voice. Of course, a newly born sheep does not immediately recognize the voice of the shepherd, but over time, because only one shepherd is leading them, all the sheep learn to recognize the voice of the one who feeds, protects, and provides for their needs. It is similar when we follow Jesus. The challenge is that we have to be intentional about listening, not just once each week, or once each day, but consistently throughout every day. We need to always keep our ears tuned to the sound of His voice because He always has something amazing to say.

There are times when we need to just be quiet and listen for a prolonged period of time. These are the moments where we grow in intimacy with our King. These are the moments when He speaks to us about the season we are in, when He discloses the plans that He has for us, when He releases the supernatural healing that we need, and so much more. There is no substitute for these times with Him, and as our relationship grows, we find ourselves dreaming about these moments, and desiring to spend even more time in His presence.

Now is a good time to pause and put listening to Jesus into practice. Find a quiet spot, close your eyes so nothing can distract you, and spend two minutes listening. Do not speak, do not respond, just listen. This may be a new concept for you, whether you are a new follower of Jesus or someone who has been following Him for a long time. Do not skip this, it is vitally important to learn how to hear His voice.

What did Jesus say to you?

_____

_____

_____

_____

_____

_____

(use another piece of paper if you need more room)

This is something you should do every day. Get this into your regular routine and you will quickly find how amazing it is to hear the voice of your King!

But listening is only part of the conversation. God wants to hear your questions; He wants to have conversations with you. You can ask Him anything, and as you learn to hear His voice, you will begin to hear responses to your questions. You can have a conversation with the creator of the universe! This is not just for certain people; it is for every follower of Jesus. It is part of your spiritual inheritance. God wants to talk to you, and He wants you to talk to Him. We have a fancy word for this, it is called prayer. But too many people view prayer as a person doing all the talking with the hope that God might be listening. The reality is that He is listening and that He has an answer for every one of your questions. It may not be the answer you expect or hope for, but it is always exactly what you need to hear. Now for some practice. Think of a question you want to ask God and write it below:

Question:

_____

_____

Now practice those listening skills and write down His answer:
Answer:

_____

_____

_____

_____

(use another piece of paper if you need more room)

That is just one example. You can ask God anything! There are some questions we often advise people to ask God on a regular basis to practice this conversation process. A great practice is to start asking questions as soon as you wake up. If you practice this, over time you will find that the very first thoughts you have when you wake up will be about God. What a great way to start the day! Here are some questions that will help you start the focus of your day in the right direction:

- Who do you say I am for today?
- What would you like me to do today?
- Is there anyone I should encourage today?

As we learn to have conversations with God, we also learn how valuable it is to simply rest in His presence. To sit quietly and allow Him to fill the space around us with His tangible presence. Have you ever noticed a shift in the atmosphere of a room when a prominent person enters? Imagine how the atmosphere would shift if Jesus walked in. The worries, doubts, and fears everyone has would melt in His presence. The amazing thing is that we can invite Him to sit with us and He will come! His presence will fill the room and cause so much peace to saturate every part of our being. Many people refer to this as soaking in His presence. It is like soaking in a bathtub. You do not have to do anything. You just sit and soak. Soak in His goodness. Soak in His grace. Soak in His healing.

How do we do this? It is simple. Just sit or lie down in a quiet place where you can be undisturbed for a few minutes. Invite God into your space and wait. Sometimes you will immediately feel the atmosphere of the room change. It is like the air becomes thicker as if you are in the middle of a cloud. Sometimes the air becomes electrified as if an electrical storm is rolling in. Regardless of what you feel or sense, taking time to sit at the feet of Jesus, and soak in His presence, is an incredibly unique way to experience His love for you. Take five minutes right now and do this yourself.

Did you experience anything new?

_____

_____

_____

_____

These are all experiential ways of developing your relationship with Jesus. This is a real relationship with a real God who wants to spend time with you! Let that idea soak in for a minute. The creator of the universe wants to spend time with you! Everything he speaks to you will always line up with what is in the Bible. Nothing He says will ever contradict the Bible, because the Bible is His word written down over the centuries to teach us more about Him. You may remember from lesson three that studying the Bible is ultimately about getting to know the author. The more time we spend in His word, and the more time we sit at His feet, the more we will know Him.

You will find, as your relationship grows deeper with God, that you will recognize His will in a lot of everyday situations. You will begin to have a supernatural understanding of things that you did not previously recognize. This is what happens as His thoughts become our thoughts and our mind is renewed to think the way He thinks. It does not mean we will always think and act perfectly but spending time with Him changes us in more ways than we may ever be able to fully understand in this life. The more time we are in His presence, the more His perspectives become our perspectives, and the more we recognize the differences between the way the kingdom of God operates and the way the kingdom of the world operates.

Putting the idea of sitting at the feet of Jesus and growing deeper in relationship with Him into a regular daily practice is the greatest action any follower of Jesus can ever take. He is and must be, the most important person in our lives. He is and must be our first love. Nothing can come before Him, and we cannot allow anything to come between us and Him. Sitting at His feet on a regular everyday basis and making this an everyday priority is the best way to maintain and grow our relationship with our King!

Video Wrap Up – Scan the QR code below to hear some final thoughts from Gene and Lauren about a common question on this topic:

Lesson Seven

Empowered by Holy Spirit

The Holy Spirit is one of the least discussed members of the Trinity in modern churches that are not charismatic in belief or denominational structure. Believers often forget that Holy Spirit is God, He is a member of the Trinity, and He has all power and authority. But He is often perceived more mysteriously and, as such, people tend to have difficulty connecting or relating to Him in the same way as God the Father or Jesus. After His resurrection, Jesus made sure the disciples were aware of the important role the Holy Spirit would play in their lives, as well in the lives of every person that chose to follow Him, and gave specific instructions before ascending to heaven:

> *Luke 24:49 – "I am going to send you what my Father has promised; but stay in the city until you have been _____ _____ from on high."*

> *Acts 1:4 – "Do not leave Jerusalem, but wait for the gift my Father promised, which you have heard me speak*

about. For John baptized with water, but in a few days you will be _____ with the Holy Spirit."

Acts 1:8 – "But you will receive _____ when the Holy Spirit comes on you; and you will be my witnesses in Jerusalem, and in all Judea and Samaria, and to the ends of the earth."

Holy Spirit empowers believers to live out their God-given purpose and fulfill the destiny given to them by God. It is the Holy Spirit who determines and releases the gifts of the Spirit that will be discussed starting in lesson fifteen. These gifts enable us to partner with God in supernatural ways to bring about healing, restoration, hope, and so much more for others. Holy Spirit has always been part of the original plan for humanity but His power working through believers was not available for everyone until after Jesus ascended into heaven. He has always been around and has always been a part of the Trinity, but we see Him take a more active role in believers' lives after Jesus returned to heaven.

Holy Spirit is seen in a variety of ways in the Old Testament even before He seemingly burst onto the scene in the book of Acts. We see Him in the very beginning of Scripture at the point of creation:

Genesis 1:2 – "Now the earth was formless and empty, darkness was over the surface of the deep, and the _____ of God was hovering over the waters."

He is there when kings and other leaders were anointed to lead the nation of Israel and when priests declared what God was speaking:

1 Samuel 16:13 – "So Samuel took the horn of oil and anointed him in the presence of his brothers, and from that day on the _____ of the Lord came powerfully upon David."

2 Chronicles 24:20 – "Then the _____ of God came on Zechariah son of Jehoiada the priest. He stood before the people and said..."

In fact, Holy Spirit was very active throughout the Old Testament. As you read through the Bible, keep an eye out for the phrase "Spirit of the Lord," "Spirit of God," or similar phrases as these typically denote the Holy Spirit. The Spirit of God is Holy Spirit. The difference in His activity before and after Jesus is that, in most situations, He came upon believers in the Old Testament, filled believers in the New Testament, and continues to fill believers today. That infilling of the Holy Spirit is described as being filled with, or baptized in, the Holy Spirit:

Acts 2:4 – "All of them were filled with the Holy Spirit and began to speak in other tongues as the Spirit enabled them."

Matthew 3:11 – "...after me comes one who is more powerful than I, whose sandals I am not worthy to carry. He will _____ you with the Holy Spirit and fire."

So, what does it mean to be baptized in the Spirit? It is an encounter with God where Holy Spirit fills you with Himself so that you can be empowered to represent Jesus and operate in the same way He did. One of the amazing promises Jesus gave to us is that we can do what He did and even greater things:

John 14:12 – "Very truly I tell you, whoever believes in me will do the works I have been doing, and they will do even _____ than these, because I am going to the Father."

The "greater things" are only possible if a believer is filled with the Holy Spirit. Everything Jesus did on earth He did as a human empowered by Holy Spirit. The only way we can do what He did is to be filled with the Holy Spirit so that we too will be empowered to boldly share the gospel of Jesus and perform signs and wonders, by His power flowing through us, that give people the healing and hope they need. This is a promise for every person who chooses to follow Jesus. You do not have to earn it. You do not have to work for it. You simply ask to be filled. Sometimes people are filled with Holy Spirit very quickly after they choose to follow Jesus. And sometimes the filling does not happen until later. Sometimes people are filled and they do not even know it! Regardless of how it happens for you, never stop asking God for this promise. He has promised to fill you and He will do it in His perfect timing.

> *Luke 24:49 – "I am going to send you what my Father has promised; but stay in the city until you have been clothed with power from on high."*

The first time this occurs in Scripture is in Acts 2:1-4:

> *"When the day of Pentecost came, they were all together in one place. Suddenly a sound like the blowing of a violent wind came from heaven and filled the whole house where they were sitting. They saw what seemed to be tongues of fire that separated and came to rest on each of them. All of them were filled with the Holy Spirit and began to speak in other tongues as the Spirit enabled them."*

Notice that the result in this passage of being filled with the Holy Spirit is that everyone in the room began to speak in other tongues. It was commonly believed for many years that speaking in other tongues was the initial evidence that someone was filled with the Holy Spirit. The assumption was that if someone did not speak in tongues, they had not yet been filled.

This position is still held by many today, but others have come to recognize there are different ways to recognize the infilling of the Holy Spirit other than speaking in tongues. This will be discussed more in-depth in chapter 23.

The ultimate purpose for the infilling is given by Jesus in Acts 1:8 before He left the earth. He specifically mentions power in this verse. The Holy Spirit entering a believer in this way empowers them to carry the gospel message into every region of the world. For some, it is to carry the gospel into their workplace or spread the news in their local communities. For others, it is to find the unreached people groups who have never heard about Jesus. Regardless of the specific mission God assigns to your life, being empowered by the Holy Spirit is the vehicle by which you are able to accomplish that mission. This infilling releases a level of boldness into the life of a believer that makes them an incredible witness to others. Jesus highlighted the importance of infilling when He told the disciples to wait in the city until it happened. Acts 1:3 tells us Jesus stayed on earth for forty days after His resurrection and Acts 2:1 tells us Holy Spirit fell on the day of Pentecost, which was ten days later. The remaining eleven disciples and some of the others who were with them devoted themselves to prayer during these ten days, but they likely would have waited much longer to receive what was promised. The question is, are you willing to wait and pray for what God wants to give to you?

We encourage you to set aside time to wait on the Lord and pray this prayer:

> Father, I thank you for your promise to fill me with your Holy Spirit. I desire to be used by you in such a way that brings Your kingdom to earth. I want to see people's lives transformed by your power. I ask you now to fill me with Holy Spirit, so I can be empowered to represent you in this world.

Write down what happens here:

_____

_____

_____

_____

_____

_____

_____

_____

Video Wrap Up – Scan the QR code below to hear some final thoughts from Gene and Lauren about a common question on this topic:

Lesson Eight

Personal Encounters with God

As you read through the Bible you will come across many accounts of the different encounters people had with God. You can also read other historical accounts of how God encountered people in the few thousand years that have passed since Jesus ascended to heaven. These stories should encourage you to pursue a personal encounter with God for yourself. God is a personal God. His desire is to spend time with His creation. His desire is for you to spend time with Him. As you spend time with Him on a regular basis, you will find yourself in His tangible presence and will have incredible encounters with Him that are designed specifically for you!

The presence of God should be explained before going any further into this lesson. Sadly, it is an element of the nature of God that many Christians only have a simple understanding of, if any at all. It is hard to understand without experiencing His presence for yourself, but once you do, you will learn to recognize when He is drawing near to you. The Bible reveals to us that God is omnipresent, which means He is everywhere at the same time. The greatness of God fills the entire universe, and even the universe cannot contain Him! It does not matter where we go, God will be there:

> *Psalm 139:7-10 – "Where can I go from your Spirit? Where can I flee from your presence? If I go up to the heavens, you are _____ ; if I make my bed in the depths, you are _____ . If I rise on the wings of the dawn, if I settle on the far side of the sea, even _____ your hand will guide me..."*

He is present everywhere, but there is a difference between His omnipresence and His manifest presence. The manifest presence of God is when you can feel Him. Sometimes it feels like a blanket has been wrapped around you. Sometimes the air around you feels thick and electrified as if you were standing inside of a cloud. There are times when you may feel intense heat, as if you are standing a little too close to a campfire, or you may feel electricity in different parts of your body. These are not the only ways to experience His tangible presence as He moves through a room, but they are some of the most common.

Have you ever been somewhere when someone of great importance entered the room? You can feel something shift in the atmosphere. The people in the room get a little excited, and it starts to create energy, or a buzz, as this important person moves through. This is similar to what happens when the manifest presence of God comes into a room. As different people start to feel Him and respond to His presence, others take notice and their hearts become excited with anticipation and a desire to encounter God in a new way. These types of encounters with God should become everyday occurrences in the life of every believer, whether you are at home, in a church service, or walking through a grocery store.

When we are intentional about spending time with Him, He shows up to spend time with us. This means you need to set aside time to spend with Jesus every day. Some people will listen to an audio Bible while they work out or while driving to work, that is OK, but it is not really being intentional. A spouse would not accept conversations on the way to work or at the gym as the primary element of the relationship, so we should not treat our relationship with God this way either. Being intentional shows that we really care about Him, what He has to say, what He thinks about a given topic, and the wisdom He wants to give us. Many people will jump at the chance to meet with a president or high-level leader and would be willing to rearrange their entire schedule to make that appointment happen. When we are meeting with Jesus, the King of the universe, the creator of all things, we need to be willing to set aside time specifically for Him. This is where the relationship grows and the encounters with Him are the most impactful. One great way to learn about encounters with God is to study past encounters recorded in the Bible. He desires to be with all of us, so let these stories encourage you to keep pursuing Him.

Moses first encountered God in the desert when he saw a bush engulfed in flames but was not being consumed by the fire.

> *Exodus 3:2-3 – "...the angel of the Lord appeared to him in flames of _____ from within a bush. Moses saw that though the bush was on fire it did not _____ up. So Moses thought, 'I will go over and see this strange sight—why the bush does not burn up.'"*

This was the beginning of many encounters Moses had with the Lord. This first one seems quite amazing, and it was, but the encounters Moses had later in life were even more profound. It was from this burning bush that God gave Moses his initial instructions about leading the Israelites out of Egypt and into the land that was promised to their forefathers. The encounter with God immediately preceded the divine direction and instruction for the rest of Moses' life. We too can receive divine instruction for our lives when we have encounters with God. Many people say that they do not know what their purpose is in life, but all they really need to know is that they can find that purpose in a supernatural encounter with their King.

Isaiah was brought up into the throne room of God in heaven and saw things that absolutely frightened him.

> *Isaiah 6:5 – "'Woe to me!' I cried. 'I am _____! For I am a man of unclean lips, and I live among a people of unclean lips, and my eyes have seen the _____, the Lord Almighty.'"*

Isaiah's initial thought after this encounter was that he was going to die. It was so powerful of a moment that he was certain his life was over. But God did not bring him to heaven to kill him, He brought Isaiah to heaven to give him an assignment. Do you see the theme in this passage? Moses received his assignment during an encounter. Isaiah also received an assignment during an encounter and was told to prophesy the words of God to the people declaring hope about their future and the coming judgment if they did not return to a lifestyle of obedience to God. His mission was not an easy one to carry out, but this encounter gave him the strength to do what the Lord required.

Some encounters, like those Ezekiel and Daniel experienced, involve interaction with angels who are also carrying out their assignments. Ezekiel had an extensively long vision where he saw many things happening in the spiritual realm. You are encouraged to read the first few chapters of Ezekiel to learn about his experience which included this piece:

> *Ezekiel 1:5-6 – "in the fire was what looked like _____ living creatures. In appearance their form was*

65

human, but each of them had four _____ and four wings."

There are many wondrous things in the spiritual realm that most humans will never see during their physical lives. Seeing these things is not the primary goal, but when we do see these things, it gives us greater context for how God operates on the earth and in the heavens. It also gives us greater faith in our own journeys knowing that supernatural beings have been sent on assignments to help us fulfill our assignments. It is important for you to remember that we are never alone!

Daniel also had encounters with God and with angels that you can read about in the last three chapters of his book. He was given visions of the distant future about nations that would rise and fall, and angels came to him to tell him what the different portions of the vision meant. In one piece, Daniel saw the Father on the throne and Jesus before he was born on the earth:

> *Daniel 7:13-14 – "In my vision at night I looked, and there before me was one like a son of man, coming with the clouds of heaven. He approached the _____ and was led into his presence. He was given authority, glory and sovereign power; all nations and peoples of every language worshiped him. His dominion is an everlasting dominion that will not pass away, and his kingdom is one that will never be destroyed."*

There are many other examples of God encounters in the Bible and, if you spend time around people who are actively pursuing God, you will hear many other stories of personal encounters they have had with God. There is even one historical account of General George Washington being visited by an angel! As you continue your journey with the Lord, you too may suddenly find yourself in the midst of the glory of God seeing things you have never seen before and hearing things you have never heard before. Do not be afraid of these encounters as they often come with direction and authority for a season of your life or for your entire life. All of us should desire every day to be in His manifest presence and should regularly ask for greater encounters with Him. We were created to be in His presence!

What is it that you desire of the Lord right now? What is it that you want Him to show you about your life, your future, or your current assignment? Ask Him now and take some time to listen, then write about your experience here:

_____
_____
_____
_____
_____
_____
_____
_____

Video Wrap Up – Scan the QR code below to hear some final thoughts from Gene and Lauren about a common question on this topic:

Lesson Nine

History of Following God

We have covered some of the foundational topics of following Jesus, but now we want to take a step back to discuss some history because you will need this context to more fully understand what we have already discussed, and what we will cover in later lessons. This will not be a long or detailed history, but rather, an overview of major events to show a thread through history that led to a need for Jesus, who is referred to in the Jewish belief system as their Messiah. Also note that the dates used in this lesson are an approximation based on the accounts of many historians and may not be accurate down to the specific year, but they will give you a close approximation of when events took place along our modern timeline.

It all begins with Adam and Eve in a garden created by God, where the original invitation to a relationship began, and the original sin took place. What is sin? Simply put, it is disobedience to God. Open up your Bible to the very beginning and take a few minutes now to read about the story of creation. You will find this in Genesis chapters 1 and 2.

Where did God place Adam and Eve?

_____

What is the one thing God told Adam and Eve they could not eat?

_____

Now continue reading about the beginning of human history by reading Genesis chapter 3.

Did you notice what the serpent did? He focused on the one thing God told Adam and Eve was off-limits and tricked them into thinking it was to their benefit to eat the forbidden fruit. His method was very subtle, and it is the same method he has used for thousands of years and continues to use today. He used this simple phrase to challenge what God had spoken, "Did God really say?" If you pay close attention, you will find that every time the enemy shows up to trick people, he often challenges the truth of what God has already spoken. This trick worked perfectly on Adam and Eve, and it continues to work perfectly on unsuspecting people today. But as we learn to recognize it, it becomes easier to dismiss.

As time went on, evil continued to spread in the world, which eventually caused God to issue a severe judgment of wiping out almost all of his creation with a worldwide flood. It is estimated that around 2460 BC, God instructed Noah to build a large ark capable of carrying his family and a portion of all animals, then once they were on this massive boat, God flooded the earth destroying the remainder of human and animal life. Noah and those with him were then responsible for repopulating the earth. Take some time now to read this story in your Bible; you will find it in Genesis chapters 6-9. Also, take note that approximately 1,650 years had passed since the creation of Adam and Eve. God's grace and mercy allowed evil to continue for a long time before he judged humanity. His mercy keeps the door to forgiveness and restoration open for a very long time, but judgment always comes at some point.

Fast forward to 2166 BC to the life of Abraham, who is the original patriarch of the Jewish faith, which is also the foundation of Christianity. Abraham is the first person we encounter in the Bible, after the flood event, who God specifically calls to follow Him. His name was Abram at the time, but God later changed it to align it with his true identity. Abraham did something that every follower of God should put into practice; take a look at this verse:

Genesis 12:4 – "So Abram _____, as the Lord had _____ him..."

Did you notice that? Abraham simply did what God told Him to do. It would not have been an easy thing to follow. Taking a journey without knowing the final destination is a big leap of faith. The faith that he portrayed is a great example of how we should live our lives today. We need to learn to simply take God at His word, trust Him wherever He leads us, and know that He will cause everything to work out for our good as long as we are obedient to Him. Abraham's faith was later tested in one of the most dramatic ways, and it is the single greatest event of his life that most people easily remember. God directed him to sacrifice the life of his son on an altar, and then at the last second, stopped him from doing so—this was a test of his total commitment to God.

Many things occurred over approximately the next 800 years, too much to cover in detail here, but the big picture details are that Abraham's line continued on, and as a result of some shenanigans with his great-grandsons and a drought that affected the entire region, his descendants ended up in Egypt. As time went on, they grew into a large number of people, and the Egyptians became afraid that their numbers would eventually become a threat, so they enslaved the Israelites for 400 years before God brought along someone to lead them out of Egypt. You should definitely read the rest of Genesis as many important things occurred during this timeframe.

Now onto approximately 1440 BC where we meet Moses, who led the Israelites out of captivity in Egypt towards the land promised to Abraham, and his descendants. Moses was born at a time when the Pharaoh of Egypt decreed that all Hebrew baby boys must be killed. His mom and her midwife hid Moses in a basket and floated him down the Nile River in hopes of escaping this cruel order. It worked, and Moses was found by Pharaoh's daughter while she was taking a bath further upstream. She adopted him and he grew up in the palace. At the age of 40, he killed an Egyptian who was beating an Israelite slave. Pharaoh sought to kill Moses for this action, and it forced Moses to flee Egypt.

Moses spent another 40 years as a shepherd until God spoke to him from a burning bush about a plan to lead the Israelite people out of Egypt and into the promised land. This plan culminated in God sending 10 plagues upon Egypt to force the Pharaoh to release them, with one final miraculous event when the Red Sea was parted revealing a dry path for the Israelites to escape Egyptian captivity for all time. After their escape, the Israelites eventually started to complain about wanting to go back to Egypt, sinned against God, and as a result were punished with 40 years of wandering in the desert until all those of the previous generation died. It was then that the military campaign to conquer all the cities and nations occupying the promised land began. Now, take some time to read Exodus chapters 1-15 in your Bible to get a fuller picture of what occurred during this pivotal time in Israel's history.

After Israel was established as a nation, sometime around 1250 BC, they went through many different periods of obeying and not obeying God. It was a bit of a teeter-totter ride as one king would lead the nation in the correct direction, and another would head off in a direction not pleasing to God. This eventually led to a situation where Israel was divided into two nations, one named the Kingdom of Israel and the other, the Kingdom of Judah. As time went on, a lot of prophecies were given warning of the impending judgment and encouraging the people to return to God, so that the judgments would not come. But the prophets were mostly ignored. As more time passed, God brought judgment against both kingdoms for disobeying Him and allowed other nations to overtake these two kingdoms. The nation of Israel fell to the Assyrians around 740 BC and the nation of Judah ultimately fell to the Babylonians around 605 BC.

The nation of Israel was dispersed into other nations, as was the commonly accepted Assyrian tradition, and we see very little reference to them anywhere else in Scripture. From a historical standpoint, they are often referred to as the lost tribes of Israel, but God knows where they ended up and where all their descendants are located today. Some historical accounts propose that they eventually migrated across what we know today as Northern Europe, but only God knows for sure. The history of the nation of Judah, however, continued in the Old Testament and they are the ones who eventually started to return to the promised land around 538 BC which led to the restoration of their temple and rebuilding of the walls around Jerusalem.

As you can easily see, the Jewish people needed someone to save them, not just from their captivity, but also from their repeated failures of following God's direction for their nation. There are a few great lessons to learn from the history of Israel. God told them it was better to live with Him as their king instead of having a human king. He warned them about what would happen if they chose to allow a human to rule the nation. But they continued to cry out for a human king anyway, so he gave them what they asked for, and we see in history that what

God warned them about is exactly what happened. We continue to see the result of those decisions today.

We also see the thread of God's grace weaved throughout the history of Israel. When they were following God wholeheartedly, he provided for everything they needed and eliminated every enemy in their path. And when they strayed from the path, He always offered forgiveness and restoration, but they did not always accept it. This is not too different from our own lives today. When we live from the perspective of following Jesus in everything we do, He leads us down the perfect path for our lives. And when we slip up or make a mistake, He is right there to offer forgiveness, brush us off, and keep us moving forward. But, like Israel, we need to be willing to make a change.

All of this led to the time when Jesus would leave His place in heaven, be born on earth as a child around 2 BC, and later begin His work of revealing Himself as God to His people. God had not given up on Israel or humanity as a whole. He came to be our Savior!

Video Wrap Up – Scan the QR code below to hear some final thoughts from Gene and Lauren about a common question on this topic:

Lesson Ten

Total Surrender

When you give your life to Jesus, you give your life to Jesus. It is not your life anymore. It belongs to someone else. It belongs to Jesus. This is a subject that many followers of Jesus struggle to fully absorb into their lives, even those who have followed Him for many years. Our human nature is to hold onto control, but Jesus has asked us to give all control to Him. We like free will. We like the ability to think and believe what we want, but when we give our life to Jesus, we surrender those rights to someone greater than us. There are many verses in the Bible that highlight this perspective:

> *1 Corinthians 7:22 – "For the one who was called in the Lord as a slave, is the Lord's freed person; likewise the one who was called as free, is Christ's _____."*

> *Mark 8:34 – "And He summoned the crowd together with His disciples, and said to them, If anyone wants to come after Me, he must _____ himself, take up his cross, and _____ Me."*

*John 14:15 – "If you love Me, you will keep My
_____."*

*Matthew 6:10 – "Your_____ come. Your
_____ be done"*

He is our King, we owe Him everything, including our allegiance and obedience. If He gives us direction, we need to follow it. If He gives us advice, we need to heed it. If He tells us to do something, we need to do it. Why? Because it is about His kingdom, not ours. It is about His will, not ours. We yield to the one who has all the wisdom, all the knowledge, and all the power. He is so much wiser than any of us can ever be, and He desired to use us to bring about an expansion of His kingdom. At the end of time, His is the only kingdom that will remain. Everything else will be gone. Our number one priority as followers of Jesus is to work towards the expansion of His kingdom. That is what really matters.

So, when He tells us to sell everything and move to a foreign country as a missionary, it is for the purpose of building His kingdom. When He tells us to give money to a particular cause, vote in a particular way, live in a particular city, or give us any other direction, it is ultimately for the purpose of building His kingdom. At the end of time, everything will fade away, and the only thing that will remain is His kingdom. Think about that for a minute. All the material possessions people work for in life will be gone. The status will be gone. The fame will be gone. The accolades and accomplishments will be gone. Only His kingdom will remain. Since this is the case, our focus should be on what He wants, and as we shift our focus in that direction, we will begin to think as He does.

Most people can accept the idea of surrender in some areas of their lives, but total surrender can be a tough pill to swallow. We can give up the stuff that we know is bad for us, but we tend to hold onto our long-held beliefs and ideas even after we give our lives to Jesus. Many followers of Jesus continue to hold onto these ideas for many years, but Jesus wants us to lay everything at His feet. That is what total surrender looks like. Every idea, every perspective, and every way of life must be laid at His feet. What happens when we do this is that we are trading up to receive His ideas, His perspectives, and His advice on how to live. The great news here is that He always has been and always will be so much wiser than all of us, so this trade is completely to our benefit.

Take a moment right now and ask God if you are holding onto anything that He wants you to give up. Ask Him if your perspective is wrong in any area of your life. Ask Him if any of your plans go against His plans. Ask Him if any of your ideas are from the world's perspective. Give it all to Him!

There are some common areas where believers tend to hold onto their beliefs instead of letting God give them His perspectives. Consider what your beliefs are in these areas and ask God if His perspective is different from yours:

Politics – people, especially in America, tend to be too focused on political parties and the politicians that are aligned with those parties. Our perspective as followers of Jesus needs to be on His kingdom above politics. This means that our votes should align with His perspectives, even if it is different from how we have always voted. We need to lay our political party affiliations and persuasions at the feet of Jesus, just like everything else. When we do this, He will give us the direction we need on who and what we should vote for—the people and things that align with His kingdom's perspectives.

Money – Jesus tells us in Matthew 6:20 to store our treasures in heaven, not on earth, and 1 Timothy 6:10 tells us that the love of money is the root of evil. But earlier in the Bible, in Deuteronomy 8:17-18, God declares that He is the one who gives the power for people to become wealthy. This can be confusing on the surface, but it is actually quite simple. The kingdom's perspective on wealth is different from the world's perspective. In the kingdom mindset, money is a tool, not a treasure. Money is an inanimate object, it is not good or evil on its own, but it can be used for good or evil purposes. We need to use the resources God gives to us as a tool to accomplish His purposes on the earth. Of course, we all need money to live, and it is very wise to save some money for larger expenses or emergencies, but we also need to put every resource we have at His feet.

Relationships – As with other things, our relationships must also be laid at the feet of Jesus. There are people who are supposed to be part of our lives, and people who are not. Some of these people will change in different seasons, so we need to be intentional about asking God who we need to be in relationship with and what level of influence should they hold in our lives. A healthy approach to this idea is that our inner circle of relationships should be those with the greatest influence and insight into our lives. This should be a smaller core group of very close friends and your spouse. Outside of that, we can have other layers of friendships that include people we know who we have not given permission to speak into our lives. Those who become a negative influence in our lives need to be removed from a position of influence until they have learned how to follow the principles of Jesus. This does not mean we shun people; it simply means that we should have healthy boundaries in place. Every follower of Jesus should also be in a relationship with someone they are accountable to who has permission to affirm, disciple, and identify areas of their life that need correction.

There are many other areas of life to consider, but these three tend to be the most common areas that are difficult for believers, even those who have followed Jesus for many years, to completely surrender. The idea here is very simple; His perspective will always be better than ours and we need to align with the greater perspective that He provides. Why? Because everything in all of creation is subject to the authority of Jesus. Every system of the world (religion, politics, etc.) is subject to change by His decree. Nothing in all of creation can hinder Him, or stop Him, from doing what He has decreed. If He said it will happen, it will happen! He is the King over everything, and He always gets the final word. Followers of Jesus need to remember this simple concept: in ALL things, we need to be aligned with what He wants, even if we do not understand it. There is no room for disagreement when you are 100% submitted to His will.

The human authors of the letters in the New Testament repeatedly refer to themselves as servants to Jesus (some translations render this as bondservants) in the opening of their letters:

Romans 1:1 – "Paul, a _____ of Christ Jesus..."
Philippians 1:1 – "Paul and Timothy, _____ of Christ Jesus..."
Titus 1:1 – "Paul, a _____ of God..."
James 1:1 – "James, a _____ of God..."
2 Peter 1:1 – "Simon Peter, a _____ and apostle of Jesus Christ..."

A servant is one who serves their master, and a great servant is one who serves their master in obedience to everything He requests or requires. We need to recognize that the biggest challenge to surrender is fear—fear that the one we surrender to is going to harm us, leave us, or in some other way mistreat us. But He has given us this promise:

Hebrews 13:5 – "..._____ will I leave you; _____ will I forsake you."

So, we can be assured that in any circumstance Jesus has our best interest at heart. We are not surrendering to an earthly ruler full of pride and manipulation who will force us to do things simply to serve His interest. We are submitting the wisest, most loving, most caring, King of the universe who knows all, sees all, and knows how to get us to the best place in life. We are surrendering to the one who created us and created a plan for our lives that we can only fulfill if we are in a relationship with Him. We are surrendering to the only one who deserves our 100% surrender. He is our first love. He is our Savior. He gave everything for us, and as we bow before Him in total surrender, He will lead us through life on the most amazing journey that only He can design. There is nothing to fear in fully surrendering to God.

Now is your chance to lay some things down that you no longer need to carry. Ask God if there is anything you are still holding that needs to be surrendered and write it here:

_____
_____
_____

Now, pray this prayer and give Him everything listed above:

Jesus, I surrender all I am to you. I lay _____ down at your feet never to pick it up again. Thank you for revealing this to me. I ask that you give me the strength and courage needed to maintain a life of total surrender to you.

Video Wrap Up – Scan the QR code below to hear some final thoughts from Gene and Lauren about a common question on this topic:

Lesson Eleven

Complete Freedom

Jesus came to earth to save us from our sins. Without Him, we could never have the forgiveness we need or the opportunity to live a life of freedom from our sinful past. Freedom can be defined in different ways, for our purpose in this lesson, freedom is defined as a state of not being imprisoned or enslaved. Everyone has a past. Everyone has something from which they need freedom. It could be addiction, unhealthy thoughts, fear, depression, and the list goes on. Sin enslaves us, but Jesus provides us freedom from that slavery, and not just temporary freedom, but complete freedom!

> *Galatians 5:1 – "It is for _____ that Christ has set us free. Stand firm, then, and do not let yourselves be burdened again by a yoke of _____."*

Take a minute right now to ask God what you need to be free from and write it here:

_____

_____

We are called to live in the world but not of the world. This requires us to separate ourselves from our past perspectives and ideas and replace them with His perspectives and ideas. The way we do this is by immersing ourselves in His presence and into His Word, the Bible. Imagine yourself immersed in a swimming pool, surrounded by nothing but water. Now imagine that water is every word God has ever spoken. That is the image we are going for here; to be fully immersed in what He has said in the past and what He is speaking to us today. This is a place we can be all day, every day. Even as we go about our lives doing all the things that we need to accomplish; we can stay immersed in this place. And when we do, the things of the world and the things of our past, no longer have an influence on our lives. Why? Because we are immersing ourselves in truth. Truth sets us free.

> *John 8:31-32 – "...If you hold to my teaching, you are really my disciples. Then you will know the _____, and the truth will set you free."*

> *John 5:4 –"..._____ born of God _____ the world."*

One of the commands God gave to the Israelites in the Old Testament drives this idea home. God instructed them to keep His commands in front of them all the time. He wanted them to constantly be thinking about His ways and His perspectives because it is the truth that would keep them from returning to their old way of thinking.

> *Deuteronomy 11:18-20 – "Fix these words of mine in your _____ and _____; tie them as symbols on your hands and bind them on your foreheads. _____ them to your children, _____ about them when you sit at home and when you walk along the road, when you lie down and when you get up.*

_____ *them on the doorframes of your houses and on your gates..."*

Many orthodox Jews still practice this literally today by tying boxes that contain God's commands on their heads and arms during their prayer time. The ultimate goal here was not to walk around with something tied to your head or hand as a constant reminder of God's commands, the goal was to get His perspectives into the hearts of His followers so that they would live according to His principles. We see this greater revelation later in Scripture through a prophecy by Jeremiah and affirmed in the Psalms.

> *Jeremiah 31:33 "...I will put my _____ in their _____ and write it on their _____."*

> *Psalm 119:11 – "I have hidden your _____ in my _____ that I might not sin against you."*

God has given us the perfect formula to be free and stay free from anything in the world that has enslaved us. That formula is to stay focused on His principles all the time. The more time we spend in His presence and the more time we study the Bible, the more we will become infused with the truth of His word. It is hard to dislodge the truth once it is firmly set in place. It becomes a strong foundation that is not easily destroyed.

> *Colossians 3:3 – "Set your _____ on the things _____, not on the things that are on _____."*

There are many different ways you can practically apply these concepts to your life; here are a few methods that work well:

Set aside time each morning to pray, worship, read the Bible, and listen to what he is speaking. Be intentional about protecting this time. Try to set aside at least an hour at the beginning of your day. This may mean that you need to get out of bed a little earlier, but it is worth it! As you do this on a regular basis, you will find that one hour is not enough. You will find yourself desiring to be in His presence even more.

Another method is to set an alarm on your watch or phone that will remind you on a regular basis to pause for a few seconds of focusing on Jesus. If you take 10 seconds every 15 minutes to thank Him throughout the day, you will find yourself thinking about Him all day long!

This idea cannot be overstated. We need to treat our relationship with our King as the most important relationship in our lives. Consider that human relationships require a lot of interaction to be healthy and successful. Someone who only spends five minutes with their spouse every day is going to find their marriage in a very difficult place; that relationship is unlikely to flourish. We cannot expect our relationship with God to flourish on the back burner—we must be intentional about spending quality time with Him every day. This is the simple process to grow into mature followers of Jesus who are able to impact the world in incredible ways. Everything with Jesus grows out of a place of intimacy with Him.

Every person has a divine purpose and calling, but that calling cannot be fulfilled outside of a deep relationship with God. God will give us gifts to use as part of our divine calling, but those gifts will not mature outside of a deep relationship with Him. Many followers of Jesus go through life without ever fulfilling their divinely given purpose because they do not understand the importance of an intimate relationship with their King. It is incredibly easy to just go through the motions by going to a church service once each week and never doing anything more with this relationship. But that is not what God wants! He wants so much more for us!

There is a great advantage to spending time with God every day. As we grow deeper into this relationship, we learn more about how He thinks, we hear His voice more clearly for ourselves and others, we see an increase in the gifts that He has given to us, we have a greater capacity for loving others the way He does, and we become more aligned with the perspectives of His kingdom. This is not an exhaustive list, but just a few of the benefits of spending time at the feet of Jesus. There really is no better place to be. Consider the words of Psalm 63:1 as a normal and healthy emotional state every follower of Jesus should have:

> *Psalm 63:1 - "O God, you are my God; _____ I seek you; my soul _____ for you; my flesh _____ for you, as in a dry and weary land where there is no water." (ESV)*

Keeping control of our thoughts is where most people start to lose the battle of maintaining freedom. It is easy to let our thoughts get out of control. It is easy to start thinking about something and end up in a place of fear, depravity, or anger. It is easy to consider the negative possibilities of life and end up in a state of depression. Our thoughts can take us to a lot of places. Sometimes, those thoughts originate in our own minds and sometimes they are inserted by the enemy. Regardless of where they come from, God has given us a strategy of how to manage each thought.

> *2 Corinthians 10:4-5 – "The weapons we fight with are not the weapons of the _____. On the contrary, they have divine _____ to demolish _____. We demolish arguments and every pretension that sets itself up against the _____ of God, and we take captive every _____ to make it _____ to Christ."*

The only thoughts we should dwell on are the ones that line up with God's perspective. If He puts a thought into our head, we should pay attention to it. If our own thoughts align with His perspective, they can stay. But thoughts that do not make the cut should be immediately thrown away. Here's a good practical tip to manage this process: anytime a thought comes into your mind that is not of God, you can simply say "that is not the voice of my Father" and dismiss it. You can take total control over the thoughts that are allowed to stay in your head.

No matter what you have struggled with in the past, no matter what you have been addicted to, no matter what has plagued your mind, there is complete freedom in Christ! As we replace the noise of the world with spending more and more time in His presence, we find the things of our past becoming a distant memory. This is something you can put into practice right now. It only costs your time, and it is completely worth every second you set aside to spend with Him. Take time right now to sit in His presence. Ask Jesus to come to sit with you. You do not have to do anything else, just sit in His presence and watch how quickly you are transformed to look and think like Him!

Take some time to lay each thing at Jesus' feet that He highlighted to you at the beginning of this chapter and write down what He gives you in return:

_____

_____

_____

Video Wrap Up – Scan the QR code below to hear some final thoughts from Gene and Lauren about a common question on this topic:

Complete Freedom

Lesson Twelve

Living with Accountability and without Compromise

Living on earth, with the variety of activities surrounding you every day, can make it difficult to stay focused on living a lifestyle that is pleasing to God. As a follower of Jesus, your life is now one that is set apart to serve Him. He is the reason for our existence and becomes the focus of our lives. This means that what He desires should become your number one priority. One of God's greatest desires is for all His followers to come into perfect alignment with the way He thinks, for our minds to be renewed according to His word, and to take on His mission of bringing His kingdom to earth.

An important part of our journey with the Lord is to go on this journey with other believers. It is unhealthy to live this lifestyle by yourself. You need other believers who can encourage you, be in community with you, share their stories of success or failure, and help hold you accountable to what God has for your life. For that purpose, you should invite spiritually healthy and mature believers to speak into your life, provide wisdom and council, lovingly point out faults, and warn you if you ever start to veer off in an unhealthy direction. Living for Jesus can become weird very quickly if we do not see it modeled well and if we do not allow those who have gone before us the permission to speak into our lives. Having someone who can walk with us on this journey gives us the benefit of their wisdom, their spiritual giftings, and their experiences. It is easy to fall for the traps of the enemy when we are by ourselves, or when we refuse wise council.

> *Proverbs 12:15 – "The way of fools seems right to them, but the wise _____ to advice."*

> *Proverbs 24:6 – "Surely you need guidance to wage war, and _____ is won through many advisers."*

Wise counselors play an important role in the life of every believer, but the idea of being accountable to someone else may feel foreign to you, especially if you have had unhealthy relationships in the past. Ask God to send you the right person who can help guide you. Ultimately you want to receive direction and guidance straight from Holy Spirit but receiving confirmation of what you believe the Holy Spirit is speaking to you is a big part of these relationships as you grow in your relationship with the Lord. This type of healthy accountability is a powerful tool in keeping us from compromising the word of God. There are many ideas in the world today that do not line up with God's perspectives, but they have become popular because people who do not understand the ways of God have created agendas based on their own hurts, anger, or past experiences. Wise council keeps us from falling into believing the world's ideas over God's ideas.

Living without compromising God's word and His desire for our life takes dedication, determination, and someone to help steer us in the right direction when we are unsure of what to do. It takes time for us to understand the ways of God as we study His word and grow in our understanding of what He requires of our lives. You will learn more about God's principles in lesson 13, but the simple underlying principle is that we serve a holy God who desires for each one of us to live a life of holiness. As you grow in your relationship with Him and discover more about the identity He has given to you, your desire for holiness will increase and your desire for the things of the world will decrease. We have been given this command from our King:

> *1 Peter 1:16 – "...Be _____, because I am _____."*

One definition of holy or holiness is to be completely separate from sin or evil conduct. Based on this definition, God is holy because He has no connection to anything sinful or evil. Another definition is to be separated to something and separated for something. As followers of Jesus, we are separated to God, meaning that we are set apart from the things of the world. And we are separated for something, meaning that we are set apart for a higher purpose in serving our King. There are creatures in heaven who have seen the fullness of God's holiness and who, right now, are declaring that holiness:

> *Revelation 4:8 - "...Day and night they never stop saying: _____, _____, _____ is the Lord God Almighty, who was, and is, and is to come."*

When we recognize the importance of His holiness and have a glimpse of even a fraction of that holiness, it changes the very core of our beliefs and thoughts, it changes the way we act, what we pursue, and how we view the world around us. For a new believer, it may feel like you are just learning to follow a series of rules to live a good life. But it is so much more than rule following. The revelation of His holiness makes you want to be more like Him. You cannot catch a glimpse of it and not be changed. You can never go back to the way you used to be or think the way you used to think after you have been given this understanding. When Isaiah saw the Lord in a vision and caught a glimpse of His holiness, it was so impactful that it scared him:

Isaiah 6:5 - "Woe to me!" I cried. "I am ruined! For I am a man of unclean lips, and I live among a people of unclean lips, and my eyes have _____ the _____, the Lord Almighty."

His holiness leads us into a greater understanding of why we need to have the fear of the Lord. You have already learned that God loves you, that He is gracious to you, that He offers you forgiveness for your sins, and these are important aspects of His nature that you need to understand. But we also need to recognize that He is God. He is the supreme ruler of the universe. There is no authority or power greater than His, and as such, He alone has the authority to judge all of humanity at the end of time, as well as to act in His best interest at any point in time. Jesus warned us of the importance of fearing God, and Solomon, many years earlier, recognized a link between this healthy fear and wisdom:

Matthew 10:28 – "Do not be afraid of those who kill the body but cannot kill the soul. Rather, be afraid of the _____ who can destroy both soul and body in hell."

Proverbs 9:10 – "The _____ of the Lord is the beginning of_____ ..."

The fear of the Lord is not the same as being afraid of God. As His children, we can approach Him with the confidence that He loves us and wants the best for our lives. We do not need to be afraid to approach Him, but we need to maintain an understanding of who we are approaching. It is a holy reverence for the creator of the universe who has invited us into an incredible relationship with Him. It is a recognition that the sacrifice that was paid for our sins was so great that we should live our lives in a way that honors His sacrifice:

1 Peter 1:17-19 – "Since you call on a Father who judges each person's work impartially, live out your time as foreigners here in reverent _____ . For you know that it was not with perishable things such as silver or gold that you were redeemed from the empty way of life handed down to you from your ancestors, but with the precious blood of _____, a lamb without blemish or defect."

Our enemy is hard at work trying to tempt you into falling for any and every type of sin that the world has to offer. He is very subtle in his tactics and very skilled at convincing humans to take the bait of compromise. It is easy to fall into that trap because the things of the world can seem very appealing on the surface and, sometimes we do not even realize that we have compromised, which is where having accountability in the form of wise counsel helps to keep us on track.

Take some time right now and ask God to reveal His holiness to you, then write down what you experience:

_____

_____

_____

_____

_____

_____

Now take a moment and ask God if there is anywhere that you have compromised, write it here, and ask for forgiveness for anything He reveals to you:

_____

_____

_____

_____

_____

Never stop pursuing His holiness. Never stop asking for a greater understanding of His holiness and for a greater measure of the fear of the Lord. Many followers of Jesus do not incorporate this elementary principle into their lives and, as a result, they fall into the traps of the devil that cause them to compromise the lifestyle God requires of each one of us. The more we incorporate the truth of His holiness in our lives, the greater impact we will have on the earth for His kingdom. When we allow Him to completely set us apart for His purposes, we put ourselves in a position of our hearts being fully committed to Him, and that is exactly what He is looking for in His followers. Make your life a constant pursuit for a greater revelation of His holiness.

Video Wrap Up – Scan the QR code below to hear some final thoughts from Gene and Lauren about a common question on this topic:

Lesson Thirteen

Kingdom Perspectives that Transform Culture

Jesus often used phrases like *"the kingdom of God is at hand,"* *"the kingdom of God has come near to you,"* or *"the kingdom of God is upon you,"* and as you read through the first four books of the New Testament you will find a lot of Jesus' teachings centered on describing different aspects of His kingdom. As you have worked through the previous lessons, you have probably already started to realize the importance of viewing everything from the perspective of the kingdom of God. This is an important concept to grasp, but one that can take some time to fully integrate into your way of thinking. Sometimes we have to unlearn what we have already learned in order to change the way we perceive everything around us.

We can easily say that the perspectives of the kingdom of God are always better than the perspectives of the world. Any idea birthed out of the systems or ideas of the world will never be able to compete with an idea that comes from the kingdom of God. Even the greatest idea in the world cannot compete with the simplest idea in God's kingdom. This will always be true. Ideas from the world may sometimes look like they are good on the surface, but what is underneath can be, and often is, very destructive. The books of 1 John and James both include strong warnings about being influenced by the perspectives of the world.

> *1 John 2:15-16 – "Do not _____ the _____ or anything in the world. If anyone loves the world, the love of the Father is not in him. For everything in the world— the cravings of sinful man, the lust of his eyes and the boasting of what he has and does—comes not from the Father but from the _____."*

> *James 4:4b – "Anyone who chooses to be a _____ of the world becomes an _____ of God."*

So, we can say that the perspectives of the kingdom of God are always better than the perspectives of the world, but an even better way to express this is to say that no idea from the perspective of the world is worth your time and should ever be considered as acceptable in the life of a follower of Jesus. Our King's perspectives should be the only perspectives we consider in any situation. This of course raises a very important question. What are His perspectives and how do I learn about each one? We find the perspectives of the kingdom in two places. First, throughout the pages of Scripture, and second, in our times of sitting at the feet of Jesus. You have already learned that studying the Bible will establish a solid foundation of these perspectives. It is also wise to share what you are learning with other more mature and seasoned Christians so they can confirm you have a clear understanding of what you are learning.

The following Scriptures are some great examples of kingdom perspectives that you can read for yourself in the Bible right now. When we know what the kingdom represents, we can use that as a litmus test for anything we encounter in life. For example, if we know that God is love, we can easily identify hatred as a perspective of the world. Read through each of these passages and think about things you have encountered in life that agree with or disagree with each one:

Matthew 6:9-10 – "This, then, is how you should pray: "'Our Father in heaven, hallowed be your name, your _____ come, your _____ be done on earth as it is in _____."

Matthew 6:33 – "But seek first his _____ and his righteousness..."

Jesus taught us to pray for the kingdom of God to come to earth and to seek His kingdom above all else!

Galatians 5:22-23 – "But the fruit of the Spirit is _____, _____, _____, _____, _____, _____, _____, _____ and _____. Against such things there is no law."

John 10:10 – "The thief comes only to _____ and _____ and _____..."

Notice the difference between the fruit of the spirit and the plans of the thief. One is the perspective of heaven and the other is the perspective of the world. The thief in this verse is a reference to religious leaders in the time of Jesus on earth who were being influenced by satan.

Philippians 4:8 – "Finally, brothers, whatever is true, whatever is noble, whatever is right, whatever is pure, whatever is lovely, whatever is admirable—if anything is excellent or praiseworthy—_____ about such things."

Matthew 22:37-39 – "Love the Lord your God with all your _____ and with all your _____ and with all your _____. This is the first and greatest

*commandment. And the second is like it: Love your
_____ as yourself."*

*Matthew 6:14-15 – "For if you _____ men when
they sin against you, your heavenly Father will also
forgive you. But if you do not forgive men their sins,
your Father will _____ forgive your sins."*

Notice that so much of the kingdom perspective is focused on loving others, living a lifestyle that is full of great attributes, not holding grudges against anyone, and even keeping our thoughts in line with these same ideas.

*Luke 6:31 – "Do to _____ as you would have them
do to _____."*

This is a powerful reminder that we should never treat someone in a way we ourselves do not want to be treated. This is true in every situation! Even if you are mistreated! Even if you are wronged! Even if you do not think the person deserves to be treated in a nice way. Revenge is a perspective of the world, not the kingdom. In everything, we respond in love and in grace.

*Mark 16:17-18 – "And these signs will accompany those
who believe: In my name they will _____;
they will speak in new tongues; they will pick up snakes
with their hands; and when they drink deadly poison, it
will not hurt them at all; they will place their hands on
_____ people, and they will get _____."*

Supernatural power that brings freedom and healing are perspectives of the kingdom. When we pray for someone, we should do so from the perspective of heaven, knowing that Jesus promised deliverance from evil spirits and physical healing of bodies. Heaven wants everyone healed! Heaven wants everyone set free!

1 Chronicles 16:23-25 – "_____to the LORD, all the earth; _____his salvation day after day. _____his glory among the nations, his marvelous deeds among all peoples. For great is the LORD and most worthy of _____ …"

The kingdom of heaven is focused on continual praise and worship of our amazing God who has invited us into an incredible relationship with Him. He is worthy of all praise!

1 Thessalonians 5:16-17 – "Be joyful _____; pray _____;"

Romans 14:17 – "For the kingdom of God is not a matter of eating and drinking, but of _____, _____ and _____ in the Holy Spirit,"

Praying continually and being full of joy are perspectives of heaven. We should be in constant conversations with our King. That is what prayer is, it is a conversation with God. Some translations render this as "pray without ceasing." We should be in constant communication with Him. Praying for five minutes each morning before heading out the door is not enough. This is the most important relationship in our life, and we must give it the attention it (and He) deserves. And we should be full of joy! 1/3 of the kingdom of God is joy. Followers of Jesus should have more joy than anyone else on earth. This is one of the perspectives of heaven.

A good practice is to ask Jesus about His perspective on any topic:

Jesus, what is your perspective on

_____?

Jesus, is there any perspective I have that is not your perspective?

What you will find is that the perspectives of the world are at war with the perspectives of God. The ideas of this world will never agree with the ideas of God because the perspective of the world is not focused on God's plans for His creation. It is important to be clear. God is not at war with Satan. Satan is no match for God and will never be able to defeat God. But the ideas that he has spread throughout the world directly challenge the ideas of God's kingdom. They are not greater than God's ideas, but humans must make a decision about which ideas they want to believe and which ideas they want to throw away. Sadly, many followers of Jesus have adopted the ideas of the world as "good" because they perceive them to be helpful. This happens because the ideas of the world can deceitfully appear to be good. But God's ideas are always better!

Video Wrap Up – Scan the QR code below to hear some final thoughts from Gene and Lauren about a common question on this topic:

Lesson Fourteen

Fallen Angels

Demons are angels who chose to rebel against God and, as a result, were cast out of heaven and no longer work to fulfill God's mission and purpose. They are responsible for all the evil in the world. Where there is chaos, you can blame them, where there is murder, you can point the finger at them, where there is any form of evil, the demonic forces are somehow involved. The chief angel who led the rebellion against God is Lucifer, and he continues to lead the demonic forces of evil to this day. He is also known by his more common name of satan. When speaking of satan, Jesus had these things to say:

> John 8:44 – "He was a murderer from the beginning, not holding to the _____, for there is no truth in him. When he lies, he speaks his native language, for he is a liar and the _____ of lies."

> John 10:10 – "The thief comes only to steal and kill and destroy; I have come that they may have life, and have it to the full." (Here, Jesus is speaking about Jewish

religious leaders but more broadly this can apply to Satan's mission).

Satan and his demonic horde will always be focused on keeping people from fulfilling their God-given purpose and destiny. They have been successful in ruining many lives and will likely be successful in ruining many more. But you are not one of those who will be ruined because you have made a choice to follow the King of kings. Satan, while he hates to see people make these decisions, does not have the power to stop Jesus from transforming lives. There is no war between God and Satan. He cannot fight God. He cannot defeat God. He is a created being and will never be able to defeat any of God's purposes. This does not mean that he and the demons do not have power. They are spiritual beings who were created for a specific purpose and, though they abandoned that purpose, they still have the power to do the things for which they were created.

God, who is all-knowing, knows every action satan will take for all of time and has already accounted for that in His plan for humanity. Satan likely knows this already, but he uses his tactics against humanity because most of humanity is unaware of how weak he is in stopping us from fulfilling what God has put us on this earth to do when we are in a relationship with Jesus. The key here is to understand the authority we have been given as representatives of Jesus on this earth, as you learned about in earlier lessons. Satan stole authority from Adam and Eve in the Garden of Eden when he tricked Eve into believing a lie with a very subtle tactic:

Genesis 3:1 – "Did God _____, 'You must not eat from any tree in the garden'?"

This has been and continues to be, a common tactic of the enemy against people. Attempting to convince people to not believe what God said to them or about them is one of his primary weapons. Remember, he is the father of lies, and lying is what comes naturally to him. He still uses this tactic today, and it has worked very well for him. Consider the mistakes you have made in your own life. If you really think about it, you will almost always find a lie somewhere near the beginning of that mistake that led you down an unhealthy path. We all have these mistakes somewhere in our past, and Jesus has set us free from the results of those mistakes but knowing that this is a common tactic of satan helps us to recognize very quickly when he is trying to deceive us again or deceive someone that we know.

This does not mean satan or a demon is hiding behind every rock. People have free will to make bad choices, sometimes based on their own evil nature, and sometimes as a result of influence from a demon. We cannot simply blame the devil for everything we do wrong. He may influence us in some way, but we still bear the responsibility of our sin, and thankfully, forgiveness is available to us through the blood of Jesus.

The great news is that Jesus took back the authority satan sole from Adam and Eve through His actions on the cross and returned the authority over the realm of the earth back to humanity.

> *Mathew 28:18 – "Then Jesus came to them and said, "_____ authority in heaven and on earth has been given to me."*

The only authority satan or demons can have in a person's life is as the result of that person inviting them in through sinful actions, or sometimes through the sinful actions of others. When we sin, we open a door of invitation to the enemy. That does not mean that someone is instantly possessed by a demon, but over the course of time, if a lifestyle of sin continues, the influence by, and control of a demonic spirit, can increase in that person's life. This is one more reason to be focused on living by the principles and perspectives of God's kingdom and avoiding the principles and perspectives of the world.

Demons are very active on the earth. They are not hiding in a hole somewhere waiting for their eventual judgment by God. They are constantly moving about the earth looking for someone to harass and for a place to gain some level of authority. They will come to you with temptations to sin, and as you grow in your walk with Jesus you will begin to recognize the difference between the voice of your Father and the voice of the enemy. They can be subtle and very convincing in their deceitful tactics, so we always have to be on guard. There are two simple actions you can take when you recognize that the enemy is speaking to you. First, you can simply tell the voice to be silent because it is not the voice of your Father. Second, you can quote Scripture that refutes the temptation being spoken to you. For example, if tempted to steal something, you can simply say "God says do not steal." Swatting away these harassments will become second nature over time.

One of the ways demons are active on the earth is through the creation of religious belief systems that keep people from knowing the truth. Every religion on the earth that is contrary to the teachings of the Bible has been birthed from a demonic influence. In his first letter to the church in Corinth, Paul shared that when people make sacrifices to different types of idols, they are actually making a sacrifice to a demon. The physical idols being worshipped were inanimate objects, but demons were also there receiving the person's worship:

> *1 Corinthians 10:19-20 – "Do I mean then that food sacrificed to an _____ is anything, or that an idol is anything? No, but the sacrifices of pagans are offered to _____, not to God, and I do not want you to be participants with demons."*

Some religious practices today continue to worship physical idols and the reality that they are actually worshipping demons is still true. Other religious practices do not incorporate physical idols, but the participants in these religions do pray to "other gods" who are actually demons pretending to be gods. Islam, for example, worships Allah, but Allah is not the God of the Bible. Allah is actually a demon pretending to be a god. When God gave the command to never worship other gods, He did so with the knowledge that no other god actually existed. So why did He give this command? Because He knew the angels He kicked out of heaven were going to pretend to be gods to receive worship from people. What we see in the Bible is the only belief system that is true. Every other religious practice is false and carries with it the danger of becoming enslaved to demonic forces.

As followers of Jesus, we have been given authority over demonic spirits who try to influence us, as well as demons who are harassing others. You learned about some of this in an earlier lesson, but here is one promise from Jesus specific to dealing with demons:

> *Mark 16:17 – "And these signs will accompany those who believe: In my name they will drive out _____..."*

You have been given authority over the demonic realm and can command them to leave anytime you encounter them in your own life or in the lives of others. This is not about fighting demons. That is not the goal. The goal is to bring people freedom, but in most situations, they have to want to be free. There's a greater degree of teaching on this subject that will not be covered here, but the simple truth is that the authority is yours, and the deeper you go into intimacy with the Lord, the more quickly demonic forces will leave when you show up. They cannot stand in the presence of God, and when we carry His presence into a place, it causes them to want to run.

Some people tend to focus on the activity of demons too much. That is not what we need to do. Our focus needs to stay on our King. If we encounter the demonic realm, we deal with it, but we do not need to go looking for demons or study their realm. The realm of the kingdom of God is where our focus needs to remain. Those angels who left their place in heaven, to rebel against God, will be judged by God at some point already fixed and determined by God. Our job as representatives of Jesus is not to go looking for demons who we can punish. Our job is to represent Him wherever we are sent with an expectation that the reality of His kingdom will show up in our midst resulting in people being healed and set free from demonic oppression.

Another important aspect for you to be aware of is that there is a hierarchy amongst the demonic forces, where some occupy positions over cities or regions, and others are more entangled with the daily affairs of humans. Everything belongs to Jesus, but the enemy tends to illegally usurp positions of authority in different regions.

> *Ephesians 6:12 – "For our struggle is not against flesh and blood, but against the _____, against the _____, against the _____ of this dark world and against the _____ in the heavenly realms."*

We have been given authority over the realm of the earth, so anything we encounter in this realm is fair game for us to take authority of and command to leave. We have not been given authority in heavenly realms, so we should not command regional spirits, who are operating outside of the realm of the earth, to leave. This is outside of the authority we have been given by Jesus and can open us up to an attack from the enemy.

> *Psalm 115:16 – "The highest heavens belong to the _____, but the earth he has given to _____."*

Most people, after learning about demonic spirits tend to wonder if there are any demonic spirits influencing their life. One easy way to find out is to simply ask God the following question. If He says yes, ask for forgiveness, renounce what He has shown you, and command the spirit to leave.

Is there any influence of the enemy in my life right now?

_____
_____
_____
_____

Dealing with demonic spirits does not need to be scary. We have been given authority, and as long as we remain in a healthy relationship with our King, we can use that authority to set people free!

You have already been forgiven of your past, so renounce any influence listed above and write down what God shows you after you are finished:

_____
_____
_____
_____
_____

Video Wrap Up – Scan the QR code below to hear some final thoughts from Gene and Lauren about a common question on this topic:

Lesson Fifteen

Gifts of the Spirit

One great advantage of being a follower of Jesus is that our relationship with our King enables us to receive gifts from the Holy Spirit which provide us with supernatural abilities that can be used in a variety of ways to bring people into an encounter with God. These gifts are available to every believer, not just for a select few, and are given by Holy Spirit in whatever way He determines. Some people are used powerfully through a few gifts while others are given different varieties of gifts. Whatever Holy Spirit gives to us is for the common good within the community of believers, referred to as the "body of Christ," as well as others we encounter in everyday life. Each of us has a particular role within the body of Christ. God chooses our role and as we commune in relationship with Him, we are given measures of gifts that also tend to increase over time.

> *Romans 9:20-21 - "...Shall what is _____ say to the one who formed it, 'Why did you make me like this?' Does not the _____ have the _____ to make out of the same lump of clay some pottery for special purposes and some for common use?"*

The second half of 1 Corinthians 12 provides great insight into how we, as members of the body of Christ, need to act in cooperation with each other, not in competition with each other. This is an important distinction. One person's calling or purpose is not more superior or less superior than another's. As we grow in maturity in our faith, we discover that God has connected us with just the right people to accomplish the mission that He has given to each one of us. The gifts of the Spirit will be covered in detail over the next several lessons, and it is incredibly important to understand, before diving into these gifts, the value each member of the body has in the kingdom of God. If you find yourself jealous of what another has, or you think of yourself more highly than another because of your giftings, you are already headed down the wrong path. The best way to approach a desire for the gifts is to ask Holy Spirit to give you what you need to accomplish your purpose on the earth.

We find a listing of spiritual gifts in 1 Corinthians 12:4-11:

> *"There are different kinds of gifts, but the same Spirit distributes them. There are different kinds of service, but the same Lord. There are different kinds of working, but in all of them and in everyone it is the same God at work. Now to each one the manifestation of the Spirit is given for the common good. To one there is given through the Spirit a **message of wisdom**, to another a **message of knowledge** by means of the same Spirit, to another **faith** by the same Spirit, to another **gifts of healing** by that one Spirit, to another **miraculous powers**, to another **prophecy**, to another **distinguishing between spirits**, to another **speaking in different kinds of tongues**, and to still another the **interpretation of tongues**. All these are the work of one and the same Spirit, and he distributes them to each one, just as he determines."*

The ultimate goal of each of these gifts is to point people to Jesus and cause them to go deeper into a relationship with Him. It will be good up front to provide a solid working definition for each of these gifts so that you understand what they mean before diving into each one individually; these are listed in an order that makes them easier to understand.

Word of Knowledge: A word of knowledge, also sometimes referred to as a message of knowledge, is supernatural information given to you by the Holy Spirit that you could not normally know through natural means about something that is currently true, was previously true, or occurred in the past.

Word of Wisdom: A word of wisdom, sometimes referred to as a message of wisdom, is supernatural insight received from Holy Spirit about a particular situation. It can also be supernatural wisdom about how to apply a word of knowledge.

Prophecy: Prophecy has been defined in many ways over the years, but the definition we will use here is that it is supernatural information given by Holy Spirit about the future;

Distinguishing of Spirits: Distinguishing of Spirits, more commonly referred to simply as discernment, is the supernatural ability to know the spirit influencing a person, system, concept, or idea. This can be a recognition of the Holy Spirit influencing something, or of a demonic spirit influencing something.

Faith: The gift of faith is the complete certainty of knowing without any doubt that God is going to supernaturally act or move in a specific way or situation.

Healing: The gift of healing is a supernatural ability to release physical or emotional healing into someone's body that results in curing a sickness, disease, or injury.

Miracles: The gift of miracles, sometimes referred to as the working of miracles, is the supernatural ability to perform miracles that are beyond human explanation.

Tongues: Speaking in tongues is the supernatural ability to speak something inspired by Holy Spirit in other human languages that you have never learned or in a heavenly language known only to God.

Interpretation of tongues: The interpretation of tongues is the supernatural ability to interpret what someone else has spoken in tongues.

We have found, through experience, that some of these gifts tend to work in tandem with others. Words of knowledge are commonly used in conjunction with prophecy or healing. Faith can also work in tandem with healing and miracles. These are just a few examples to provide foundational descriptions that give you a framework for how Holy Spirit can use you to represent Jesus in a fuller way on the earth. The following lessons will dig deeper into each of these gifts to give you a fuller understanding, and you can refer to this lesson as needed to refresh your memory on each of these definitions.

Video Wrap Up – Scan the QR code below to hear some final thoughts from Gene and Lauren about a common question on this topic:

Lesson Sixteen

Words of Knowledge

Words of knowledge are most commonly used today as a way to identify people who are in need of physical or emotional healing, highlight someone for the purpose of prophecy, or encourage someone by showing them that God cares about their situation, usually resulting in salvation. We have a few examples of Jesus using words of knowledge in the Bible:

> Jesus' interaction with the woman at the well in John 4:1-42 is a great example of a word of knowledge. Take a minute to read this passage and, as you do, you will notice that Jesus pointed out something from her past (*five husbands*) and something currently true (*living with someone who is not her husband*).

> The interaction Jesus had with Nathaniel in John 1:43-50 is another great example of a word of knowledge. Jesus "saw" him under a fig tree (*past event*) before Phillip went to tell him about the Messiah. He did not see him with his physical eyes but saw him through a word of knowledge.

Experientially, we have also learned that words of knowledge can be received in a variety of ways. It is not always the same for everyone, so you will need to learn how God speaks specifically to you as you continue on this journey with Him, but in the area of healing, the following methods, which have been taught since the mid-1980's are six of the most common ways people have experienced Holy Spirit giving them words of knowledge:

Feel it – in this category, people feel pains or other sensations in areas of their body where someone else has some type of physical injury or problem. It can manifest as a quick sharp pain, vibration, intense heat, or in other ways. Usually, it is a quick pain or sensation and then it is gone, so you have to get used to paying attention to random pains and you have to be able to distinguish between your own pain and what may be a word of knowledge. For example, you may be having a conversation with someone and then feel a sudden quick pain in your left knee that lasts for about 2 seconds. This could be a word of knowledge for the person you are talking to and a sign that God is going to heal their knee injury. This is a very common way many people receive a word of knowledge for healing.

Read it – in this category, words will supernaturally appear on a person, on a wall, on the floor, or anywhere else you may be looking. The words usually appear to be floating in the air in front of someone or something and are only seen by you. For example, you could be in a room full of people and suddenly see the words "drug addiction" appear on a wall. This is a word of knowledge that someone in the room is dealing with this issue and God wants to supernaturally free them from addiction.

See it – in this category, people will see something stand out about a person, see an image in their head about a particular scenario, or even have a vision of something that previously occurred. For example, you could be looking at someone and suddenly their ear looks like it is 5 times larger than normal. This could be a word of knowledge that God wants to heal their ear. An image of an intricately designed gold ring may suddenly pop into your head. This could be a word of knowledge about God wanting to have an encounter with a person wearing this intricate ring.

Dream it – this category is basically the same as see it except that it occurs while a person is sleeping and can include a lot more detail than what may occur with a quick mental image. For example, someone may dream about a red car that was involved in an accident and a person having a back injury as a result of that accident. This could be a word of knowledge about God wanting to heal someone who was involved in that situation. It is important to write these types of dreams down so you know who to look for when the time comes to use that word of knowledge.

Think it – this category is similar to see it, but usually involves more words than images. For example, you may be sitting at a coffee shop and suddenly the phrase red dress and blue shoes pops into your head. It is likely that this is a word of knowledge and that God has a message or healing for someone who fits that description. This can be one of the most difficult ways to discern a word of knowledge and is also one of the most common.

Speak it – this category is likely the strangest in that a person suddenly says something they were not thinking or talking about. For example, you may be talking to a friend, or speaking to an audience, and suddenly the phrase "God is going to heal someone with fibromyalgia" comes out of your mouth. This is a word of knowledge that someone is dealing with this problem, and that God is about to heal it.

Words of knowledge can also be used in conjunction with the gift of prophecy. When this happens, the see it, dream it, think it, or speak it categories are typically the way the word of knowledge is given, and it precedes or is interwoven with a prophecy. For example, you may be speaking to a group of friends and then suddenly see a blue house with the address of 1234 River Road in your mind. You then ask your friends if that address means anything to them, and one friend says, "that was my address when I was a kid." This is a word of knowledge about something from their past and a sign to you that God wants you to minister to them in some fashion.

All of these categories and examples can also be used when talking with non-believers about Jesus. You can receive words of knowledge about their lives, physical injuries, past or current situations that need to be resolved, or many other things. These are all signs that God wants to have an encounter with the person you are talking with, shows them that God is real because there is no way you could naturally know what has been revealed to you, and can lead to the person choosing to give their life to Jesus.

Each of these categories and examples are ways we commonly see God work through the gift of words of knowledge, but they are not limited to just these areas. God is incredibly creative and can use anyone in any way He wants. While on your journey with Jesus, you will discover the unique ways He speaks to and through you. As Holy Spirit gives different supernatural gifts to you, you will also learn how to partner with Him to bring people healing, freedom, encouragement, and anything else Jesus wants them to have. It requires some risk, but the risk is completely worth it when there is an opportunity to see someone's life touched in a supernatural way.

Now for some practical application. What do you do when God gives you a word of knowledge for someone, or at least when you think you have a word of knowledge? There are a few different ways to approach this, and many people blend their own personality and style into it as they become more confident in the idea of partnering with the Holy Spirit. A minister standing in front of a crowd of people might rattle off a list of words of knowledge they received by simply saying "someone here has an injury in their left shoulder," "someone here was involved in a car accident 3 years ago," or something similar depending on what Holy Spirit has revealed. This is an effective method for a larger group of people because it gives the opportunity to minister to many people at once.

Another great method that is very effective, and very natural, in one-on-one situations, is to ask questions. As you receive a word of knowledge, you can simply ask the person you are with if it applies to their life. The only way you will know if you are hearing Holy Spirit correctly is if you take a step of faith and test out what you are feeling, sensing, etc. Here are a few ways you could start this conversation:

- Were you ever in a situation where...?
- Did you ever have a problem with...?
- Is there any kind of injury in your...?
- Did you ever own...?
- Did you ever live in ...?

The great thing about this method is that, if you are wrong, you can easily explain it away without feeling completely foolish. When ministering to people individually, we have found that asking a question, such as one listed above, often leads to miraculous healing within a few seconds. Here's a great example of this:

> "I was talking with a few guys when I suddenly felt a sharp pain in my left knee. I knew that there was nothing

wrong with my knee, so I asked if any of them had a problem with their knees. The one standing directly in front of shared that he was currently dealing with an injury in his knee, so I prayed for it, and God healed him on the spot."

It really is as simple as taking a small amount of risk, asking a question, and watching to see what God does next. It can be unnerving at first, to explain to someone that you think God is telling you something about their life, but if you consider the possibility that a miracle may occur, that someone's life may be radically changed by God for the better, it is worth ANY amount of risk. We will cover how this gift works with prophecy and wisdom in a later lesson to give you more practical application. The key in all of this is to listen, practice, and listen some more. Take the risk, it is totally worth it!

Take a moment to ask God to release this gift into your life and write down what you experience:

_____

_____

_____

_____

Return to this space in a few weeks to record any words of knowledge you have received and what happened after you prayed for someone:

_____

_____

_____

_____

Video Wrap Up – Scan the QR code below to hear some final thoughts from Gene and Lauren about a common question on this topic:

Lesson Seventeen

Healing

One of the things we love about supernatural healing is that many times, it can be immediately tested to see if the person in front of you is better than they were before you prayed. Many of the other spiritual gifts cannot be immediately tested. Prophecy, for example, can only be tested over time to see if it was true. But, unless the miracle involves something internal to the body, healing can usually be tested on the spot. This can be both nerve-racking and exhilarating at the same time. It is exciting to see someone supernaturally healed, but sometimes we get nervous because we do not know if anything is going to happen when we pray. Understanding the will of God can help build our faith which leads to greater expectation, so we will start with the Scripture that shows us Jesus paid for our healing:

> *Isaiah 53:5 – "But he was pierced for our transgressions, he was crushed for our iniquities; the punishment that brought us peace was on him, and by his _____ we _____."*

Healing is available to us, as followers of Jesus, because He paid for it as part of His sacrifice. That is a foundational truth. But healing is also available to those who have not yet chosen to follow Him. We see throughout the books of Matthew, Mark, Luke, and John that Jesus healed everyone who came to Him. Notice the word "all" in the following verse:

Matthew 8:16 – "When evening came, many who were demon-possessed were brought to him, and he drove out the spirits with a word and healed _____ the sick."

Jesus never turned anyone away. He never told anyone that it was not His will to heal them. He never told anyone that it was not their time. He consistently healed everyone who came to Him. So, we can confidently say that it is ALWAYS God's will to heal. Even if it does not happen, that does not change the fact that it is His will. That may sound contradictory on the surface, but it requires a shifting of our perspective into a kingdom mindset to realize that God's will is always good, though sometimes His will is not accomplished on the earth. Keep the idea that God's will is always to heal in your mind and let God show you how true it is as you progress on this journey.

As we read through Matthew, Mark, Luke, and John, we see that healing was a regular part of the life and ministry of Jesus. It seems that everywhere He went, someone was in need of healing, and He repeatedly healed the ones who were in need. But then we see an interesting thing take place in Matthew chapter 10:

Matthew 10:1 – "Jesus called his twelve disciples to him and gave them _____ to drive out impure spirits and to _____ every disease and sickness."

Matthew 10:8 – "_____ the sick, raise the dead, cleanse those who have leprosy, drive out demons. _____ you have received; _____ give."

Jesus was not keeping this healing power all to himself. He wanted His followers to do the same things He was doing. He wanted His followers to be an extension of His ministry, not just while He was physically on the earth, but even after He returned to heaven. The disciples were sent out to heal those who were sick, and before Jesus returned to heaven, He gave us another vital piece of information:

> *Mark 16:17-18 – "And these signs will accompany _____ _____: In my name they will drive out demons; they will speak in new tongues; they will pick up snakes with their hands; and when they drink deadly poison, it will not hurt them at all; they will place their hands on _____people, and they will get _____."*

The authority to heal was not just for the twelve disciples to put into practice, it is for everyone who believes. We all get to participate in the ministry of Jesus to heal the sick. It is not set aside just for certain people who are chosen by God to have a healing ministry. It is for every believer. How do we know this to be true? First, because, as we have already seen, the Bible says it! That is the most important piece. And second, we see supernatural healing occur so frequently through the lives of believers that it proves this statement in the Bible to be true. Here are a few examples:

> *Acts 9:32-34 – "As Peter traveled about the country, he went to visit the Lord's people who lived in Lydda. There he found a man named Aeneas, who was _____ and had been bedridden for _____years. "Aeneas," Peter said to him, "Jesus Christ heals you. _____ and roll up your mat." Immediately Aeneas got up."*

> *Acts 14:8-10 – "In Lystra there sat a man who was _____. He had been that way from _____ and*

had never walked. He listened to Paul as he was speaking. Paul looked directly at him, saw that he had faith to be healed and called out, "_____ on your feet!" At that, the man _____ up and began to walk."

Acts 8:6-7 – "When the crowds heard Philip and saw the signs he performed, they all paid close attention to what he said. For with shrieks, impure spirits _____ of many, and many who were paralyzed or lame were healed."

Notice here that Paul was not one of the original twelve disciples of Jesus, and yet God used him in powerful ways. These verses are just a few examples of how God has used people in the past. You can be used in powerful ways as well. You have the opportunity to partner with the King of the universe and participate in what He wants to do on the earth and in the lives of other people. Take a minute to think about people you know today who need a supernatural healing miracle and write their names below:

_____

_____

_____

_____

_____

Now, think about how their life would change if they received the miracle they need. Think about what it would be like if God used you to bring healing to their life. How amazing would that be? It is not impossible. In fact, as a follower of Jesus, it is actually very probable!

The way we need to view supernatural healing is very simple; Jesus promised that when those who believe in Him lay hands on sick people, they will get well:

Mark 16:17-18 - "And these signs will accompany those who believe: In my name they will drive out demons; they will speak in new tongues; they will pick up snakes with their hands; and when they drink deadly poison, it will not hurt them at all; they will _____ their _____ on sick people, and they will get _____."

There are some other promises in these verses as well, but for now, stay focused on the healing piece. Jesus promised it, so our job is to put it into practice. This is faith in action, this is simple faith in believing that what Jesus said is true.

So, here is a simple and practical method, developed by Dr. Randy Clark, that you can use to pray for anyone who needs any type of healing:

1. Ask the person what needs to be healed.
2. Ask the person what level of pain they are in (0-10) or if there is any reduction in range of motion.
3. Pray
4. Ask the person to test it out, see if the pain has reduced, see if the range of motion has increased, etc.
5. Pray again, if necessary.

This model is a great way to put praying for healing into practice. We do not always have to do it this way, but this is a great way to get started. Why do we ask about the pain level or range of motion? Because it is an easy thing to test out after we pray. If the pain goes down, or the range of motion improves, it is a sign that God is doing something, and we should keep praying. After each prayer, we can have them test it out again to see if there is continued improvement. Step three says to pray, and how we pray is also very important.

Praying, in the context of healing, is a little different than how we may normally talk to God. In this sense, we are not asking God to heal the person, we are commanding the body to be well based on the authority that God has given to us. It does not have to be a long laborious process, we can make simple declarations, or give simple commands, and then have the person test out what is happening. Here are a few example ways you can put this into action when you encounter someone who needs supernatural healing:

"Back be healed in the name of Jesus."
"Pain get out."
"Cancer cells, die right now."
"Disease, get out of this body."

It really is that simple! When God speaks, something happens. He does not have to spend a long time talking about it. He simply commands it to be so, and it is so! We are His representatives on the earth, and we can operate in the same manner. Why, because we get to participate in His divine nature:

> 2 Peter 1:4 – "Through these he has given us his very great and precious promises, so that through them you may participate in the _____, having escaped the corruption in the world caused by evil desires."

Here's a scenario to help you have a fuller understanding of how you can use this prayer model to get started praying for healing right away:

Greg is walking down the street and he sees his friend, Marcus, limping while he walks. Greg walks over to Marcus and says, "Hey, Marcus, what's going on with your leg? Why are you limping?" "I tripped over some steps the other day, twisted something, and now it hurts to walk," Marcus replied. "How much pain are you in, on a level from 1 to 10?" asks Greg. Marcus says, "Oh, probably about a 6 or 7."

Notice here that Greg has already gone through the first 2 steps of the prayer model in a very natural conversational way.

Greg then said, very confidently, "I can help you get rid of that problem!" Marcus, with a puzzled look on his face, said "what do you mean by that?" "I'm going to pray for you, and God is going to heal you, right now," says Greg. Then Greg kneeled down right there on the sidewalk, placed his hands on Marcus' knee, and in a normal tone of voice said, "knee, I command you to be healed in the name of Jesus!" Greg continued, "all pain go right now, full mobility be restored right now!" "OK," Greg said, "Walk around and see if it feels any better."

Notice here that Greg has now finished step 3 and has moved to step 4.

Marcus walked about five feet away from Greg, spun around, and walked back towards him, without any limping or grimacing. He now wore a big smile on his face as he proclaimed, "The pain is all gone, it feels great!"

In this scenario, Greg and Marcus are friends, so Greg took the liberty of just praying without asking for permission. If you do not know the person or do not know them well, you should ask for permission to pray and to lay hands on them. Now, you may be wondering, "what do I do if nothing happens?" That is a common question and the way we approach it is also very simple. We encourage the person to keep praying and that it is God's will to heal them. We want them to feel loved and encouraged no matter what happens. If someone feels loved and encouraged, you have done your job!

It is important to remember that Jesus inaugurated the coming of His kingdom, and until He returns again, we live in the space of the kingdom now and not fully yet. We believe that God wants to heal everyone, no matter what happens, and also recognize that there is a mystery to why some people are not healed. Now it is your turn to put this into action, go find someone to pray for, and watch how quickly God starts to use you to bring them the healing that they need!

Take a moment to ask God to release this gift into your life and write down what you experience:

_____

_____

_____

_____

Return to this space in a few weeks to record any encounters of what happened after you prayed for someone:

_____

_____

_____

_____

Video Wrap Up – Scan the QR code below to hear some final thoughts from Gene and Lauren about a common question on this topic:

Lesson Eighteen

Distinguishing of Spirits

The supernatural gift of distinguishing of spirits, sometimes referred to as discernment of spirits, or simply discernment, is one that gives a believer insight into what type of spirit is influencing a person, idea, system, nation, etc. It is a powerful gift that reveals an element of the spiritual realm which is unable to be seen or observed in this way without the Holy Spirit providing this particular gift. For simplicity's sake, we will refer to this gift as "discernment" throughout this lesson. Those who have the gift of discernment are able to know and recognize, by supernatural means, if a good or evil spirit is involved in a situation, as well as if neither is present.

The spiritual realm is a topic of discussion and training all by itself that will not be discussed in detail here, but the spirits that occupy this realm can be broadly categorized as good or evil. Satan and his demons are the spiritual beings that fall into the evil category. As discussed in lesson fourteen, they were formerly angels who rebelled against God and were kicked out of heaven as a result. They are defeated enemies of God who spend their time harassing people, causing chaos, and influencing death and destruction everywhere they go. It is important to note here once again that there is no war between God and Satan. Satan is defeated. He knows he is defeated. There is no question in his mind about the power and authority of Jesus. He is only successful in his operations because people are easily manipulated and deceived. This is why spiritual discernment is such an important gift.

Angels are spiritual beings that fall into the category of good. Of course, God is also in this category, but He has already been covered in an earlier lesson. There are also other heavenly creatures discussed at times in the Bible who fall into this category, but they will not be covered in this lesson. Angels carry out their God-given missions in a myriad of ways to help followers of Jesus fulfill their own God-given purpose. Angels mostly go about unseen with many people unaware that they are present with them in many situations. As you study the Bible you will come across many situations where angels interacted with humans to help them accomplish their missions, provide supernatural protection, and even challenge those who were headed in the wrong direction. So, angels, like humans, have a particular role to play in God's plan for humanity and they carry out many different functions according to that role. Two particular Bible verses give us a partial definition and description of angels:

> *Psalm 103:20 – "Praise the Lord, you his angels, you mighty ones who do his _____, who obey his word."*

> *Hebrews 1:14 – "Are not all angels ministering spirits _____ those who will inherit salvation?"*

The human spirit is an additional category but is different from what has already been presented because, in this area, discernment can reveal the intentions of a person's heart, what they are thinking or feeling, and can distinguish between these things apart from the influence of any other spiritual force. This gift can reveal when someone is feeling depressed, lonely, etc. apart from having a demonic spiritual influence in these areas. Jesus demonstrated the distinguishing of the human spirit when He encountered Nathaniel:

> *John 1:47 – "When Jesus saw Nathanael approaching, he said of him, Here truly is an Israelite _____ there is no deceit."*

A person who has the gift of discernment, whether they are discerning a good or evil supernatural spirit, or the human spirit, is gifted to minister and give advice to people, especially in the areas of hope and freedom. They minister hope by revealing the activity of God or angelic beings in a believer's life, give advice for situations where they are able to discern if God or the enemy is behind a particular situation or system, and freedom through the removal of evil spiritual influences. The distinction between angels and demons is an important one to recognize. Demons are actively engaged in causing trouble for humanity. Angels, on the other hand, are actively working to help humanity as well as to fulfill God's mission on earth. Demons manipulate people to do all sorts of evil. Angels never engage in manipulative practices to accomplish their mission. There are many verses throughout the Bible that highlight ministering in hope and freedom, here are two of them:

> *2 Kings 6:16 – "And Elisha prayed, "Open his _____, Lord, so that he may see." Then the Lord opened the servant's eyes, and he looked and saw the hills full of horses and chariots of fire all around Elisha."*

> *Mark 9:25-27 – "When Jesus saw that a crowd was running to the scene, he _____. "You deaf and mute spirit," he said, "I command you, come out of him and never enter him again." The spirit shrieked, convulsed him violently and came out. The boy*

looked so much like a corpse that many said, "He's dead." But Jesus took him by the hand and lifted him to his feet, and he stood up."

God gives us these spiritual gifts for a reason. People who have this particular gift are commonly used by God to regularly bring freedom to those who are being tormented by the devil. This is not the only way they are used, but it is a common way. The ability to distinguish between spirits does not mean that someone who has this gift should point out everything they see. Those who operate at a high level in this gifting tend to see spiritual activity on a regular basis and it would be difficult for them to minister to every person they encounter who needs freedom. Some people are not ready to be free. Some people have actively invited demonic spirits into their lives because they think it gives them some type of power or influence; religious practices that involve casting spells is a good example of this situation. Because everyone is in a different place, it is extremely important to constantly be listening to Holy Spirit and only take action on what He says to do. Ministering to someone who has some form of demonic influence is outside the scope of this discipleship guide, but it is something you should study at a later time, especially if God calls you to that arena.

If Holy Spirit has already given you this gift, or if He gives it to you in the future, it would be good to know how to practically use it in different situations, how to respond to what you are discerning, and how this information is typically recognized. Generally speaking, if you have a gift of discernment, you will know and recognize things without understanding why you know. It can be a little disconcerting at first, but over time, as you practice using the gift, it will become more natural and normal to receive this information from Holy Spirit. For example, you may look at someone and recognize that a demonic spirit is causing them to be depressed. Or you may look at another person and recognize the joy of the Lord resting upon them. You may even discern whether or not a particular idea or system is good or evil.

How you discern specifically could come as a result of seeing something with your eyes, sensing it within your spirit, or hearing the Holy Spirit speak it to you. There is a lot of variety and creativity in the way the Holy Spirit uses believers in the area of spiritual giftings, so you will need to learn to flow with however He uses you; this is true of all spiritual gifts. Sometimes you will discern an influence but will not recognize exactly what it is. Regardless of what you see, or who you see it on, there are three great questions you can ask Holy Spirit that will give you the understanding you need:

- What is this thing that I am discerning?
- Why are you showing this to me?
- What action do you want me to take?

If Holy Spirit tells you to share what you are seeing, it is best to have a one-on-one conversation with the person so that they do not feel embarrassed. It is also good to ask if they want to know what you are discerning so that you have permission to speak into their life. This is an honoring way to use a gift of discernment and helps us stay humble. One great way to practice using this gift when first starting out is to only share the good things that you see as a way to encourage those around you.

As this gift of discernment grows, you will more easily recognize common spiritual influences and may even begin to discern what is happening in people's lives everywhere that you go. This is not a gift limited to just a church setting; if it has been given to you, you can use it everywhere you go. As it grows, you will learn more about the unique way God speaks specifically to you through this gift and will easily be able to turn it on or off depending on the situation. You will always have more questions than answers, and that is OK, as you will be receiving supernatural information from our supernatural God who knows and sees everything. There are also a few warnings you should heed because a person with a gift of discernment can easily go down a path of using this gift in a negative way:

- Do not judge people when you see something negative
- Do not use this information to manipulate people
- Do not gossip about what you are seeing

This is a vitally important gift that is needed within the body of Christ to help believers stay healthy in their spiritual journeys and to bring freedom to so many who are oppressed by the devil. It is not an easy gift to carry, as you have to learn how to protect the information God is giving to you, but it is one that can quickly destroy demonic strongholds when used with love and humility. Ask Holy Spirit today if this is a gift He wants to give to you!

Take a moment to ask God to release this gift into your life and write down what you experience:

_____
_____
_____
_____

Return to this space in a few weeks to record anything you have discerned in the spirit realm since praying this prayer:

_____
_____
_____
_____

Video Wrap Up – Scan the QR code below to hear some final thoughts from Gene and Lauren about a common question on this topic:

Lesson Nineteen

Words of Wisdom

Who is the wisest person you know? Who is the one person on earth you could go to for advice and input about any situation you are facing? There are people who have a lot of knowledge about different topics, which is essentially information about a concept, person, or object, but wisdom is a little different. It has been defined in many different ways, but it is essentially the ability to apply insight and perspective about something. Wisdom is not simply knowing a lot about a lot. It is bigger, it provides context and action. An astronomer can tell you about the moon, but only an astronaut who has walked on the moon can give you advice about how to prepare for such a task. This is because human wisdom is typically based on experience, which is why the older a person gets, and the more they experience in life, the more wisdom they have to give away.

The spiritual gift of wisdom, or word of wisdom, is different because rather than being based on human experience or a human perspective on how to apply knowledge to a situation, this wisdom can only come as supernatural insight from God. This is greater than any other wisdom in all the universe. No person can ever match the wisdom of God. No person, even if they lived for 1,000 years would ever be able to provide the breadth and level of insight that God can give. He is the creator of knowledge and wisdom. Wisdom does not exist without Him. In fact, we see in Scripture that wisdom was established sometime before or during the creation of the earth:

> *Proverbs 8:23 – "I was formed _____ ages ago, at the very _____, when the world came to be."*

A word of wisdom is the supernatural insight given by Holy Spirit to, or through, a person for a particular situation. It is God's wisdom for a situation, which automatically makes it the greatest wisdom anyone can receive. Those who operate in this gift are able to give supernatural advice for situations or circumstances that, if followed, bring about the best end result. This is because God's wisdom can provide a solution to any problem in a way that human wisdom can never provide. Remember, this is not human wisdom born out of the human experience, and it is not the same as being naturally wise, it is God's wisdom for the moment.

You may find yourself in a situation where you do not know what action to take, or how to resolve a particular problem. Where humans cannot see a way out, God can see the perfect path to take. In these situations, ask God for His wisdom in the situation, and seek the counsel of other believers who operate in this word of wisdom gifting to see if God will provide greater insight to you through their prayers. It is a valuable thing to know who in the body has different giftings, so you know who to go to in a time of need. God provides the answers, but He often uses people as part of the process.

Practically speaking, a word of wisdom typically manifests similarly to prophecy while someone is speaking what they hear Holy Spirit speaking. Sometimes this is after a period of seeking the Lord in prayer, and sometimes it just comes out of the mouth without even thinking about the situation. There are also times when a word of wisdom will come immediately after a word of knowledge. In these cases, it is the wisdom of what to do with the word of knowledge that was just received. This is not common when receiving words of knowledge for healing but can happen when Holy Spirit gives a word of knowledge about a particular situation a person is dealing with at the moment.

When we are in sync with Holy Spirit, He will speak to us and through us in ways that we could never imagine. It is amazing what God will do through those who are in a relationship with Him. Even in times of trouble, we have a promise that we can rely on Holy Spirit to give us the right words to speak, as we see in this passage:

> *Matthew 10:19-20 – "But when they arrest you, do not worry about what to _____ or how to say it. At that time you will be given what to say, for it will not be you speaking, but the _____ of your Father speaking through you."*

A word of wisdom is not just for a solution to a problem. It is also for direction and guidance in our everyday walk with Jesus. As you continue to follow Jesus you will learn to trust His voice when He speaks to you, and you will learn that His direction and guidance are always the best for our lives. He has your best interest at heart and would never lead you in a direction that is bad. Sometimes His wisdom will come directly to you, and sometimes He will give others a word of wisdom through a supernatural gift they are operating in to keep you moving in the right direction for your life's calling.

This revelatory gift is important to the body of Christ and is needed, perhaps more in today's environment, than ever before. We are living in a time where many people are choosing to live, not just by the world's wisdom, but with a complete disregard for any wisdom at all as they choose to do what makes them feel good with a "you only live once" attitude. A word of wisdom released at the right moment to a person seeking advice can turn them in a new direction very quickly. Ask Holy Spirit to release this gift to you and start listening more intently for His wisdom. Solomon, who was supernaturally given wisdom by God, had this to say:

> *Proverbs 4:5 – "Get_____..."*
> *Proverbs 4:7 – "The beginning of_____is this: Get*
> *_____."*

And when we get to the New Testament, we see that God created this supernatural gift so the body could be blessed and encouraged with His wisdom. The wisdom of man can only take us so far. We need supernatural wisdom from the throne of God to navigate all that He wants us to accomplish on the earth.

You may be in a situation right now that requires the wisdom of God in order to navigate it correctly, or you may need supernatural advice for the next steps to take in life. Take a few minutes to ask God for His wisdom and write down what he says here:

_____

_____

_____

_____

_____

_____

Video Wrap Up – Scan the QR code below to hear some final thoughts from Gene and Lauren about a common question on this topic:

Lesson Twenty

Hearing the Voice of God

Do you know that you can hear God speak to you? If you have chosen to follow Jesus, you have a guarantee that you can hear and recognize His voice when He speaks to you! Learning to recognize when God is speaking is an important and valuable lesson because when we can clearly hear what He has to say, we can receive direction for our lives, insight into perspectives that we need to change, answers to questions, and ultimately, actively participate in our relationship with Him. Some of this was practiced in lesson six, and this lesson will take the idea of hearing God speak to a deeper level.

Talking to God is as simple as talking to another person. We do not need to complicate it and we do not need to make it weird. When you are with a friend, you naturally talk about different things, ask each other questions, share stories, and have different conversations. You can talk to God in the same way. He is always listening to what you have to say. Maybe you never thought about that before. Maybe you have thought that God does not care about what you think or is too busy to take the time to listen to you. Neither of those thoughts are true. He is always listening. Take a moment right now and write down a few questions you would like to ask God:

_____

_____

_____

_____

_____

_____

_____

When we have a conversation with God, we must include time to listen. Often when we pray, we tend to talk a lot about all the things we want or need and then move on without ever taking time to listen to God's response. So, the first thing you need to learn about hearing God's voice is the importance of listening. It is good to make this a regular part of your prayer time. Be quiet, be still, and just listen. You may be surprised how quickly you hear Him speak and what He says to you. There is no one wiser we can listen to. There is no one with better advice than Him. There is no one worth spending time with more than our King. As we listen, we should remember this simple promise Jesus gave us. You are one of His sheep if you have chosen to follow Him:

> *John 10:27 - "My sheep _____ my _____, and I know them, and they follow me."*

Imagine you are sitting in a room and someone sitting twenty feet away is talking to you. How well can you hear them? How easily will you be able to understand what they are speaking? You probably will not hear much at all unless they move closer to you. Now consider that when you draw close to God, you will be able to hear Him more clearly. Some have used the analogy that God whispers to us because it forces us to draw close to Him to hear what He is saying. One of the easiest ways to draw close to God is through worship. God loves our praise, and He draws near to us when we spend time in a place of praise and worship. This makes it much easier to hear His voice.

So, start by spending time praising Him. God's presence often fills the atmosphere around us when we spend time praising Him. This is not a chore. It is not a simple act of obedience. This is our outward expression of how much we love and appreciate our King, it is a declaration of how good He is, how He has done amazing things, and how much we desire to be with Him. When your praise flows from a place of love and adoration from God it becomes more than just the words of a song. It becomes an attractive aroma to our King and attracts His presence to us. It is an amazing thing to be in the presence of God, and it is a place where we can hear His voice very clearly.

You may remember learning about the presence of God in an earlier lesson, now we will dive a little deeper. God is everywhere at all once; we call this omnipresence. But there is something different between His omnipresence and His tangible presence. When the atmosphere of a room fills with the presence of God, you can feel it in a variety of ways. Sometimes it feels like the air has become thicker and that someone wrapped a large heavy blanket around you. Sometimes His presence causes a heightened emotional state of joy, love, excitement, or many other emotions. Sometimes recognition of His power and holiness sweeps through the minds of the people in the room causing them to bow on their knees in reverence. Sometimes the air feels electrified, and you can feel small currents of electricity flowing over your body. There are many different manifestations of God's presence, and as you spend more time in worship you will begin to experience His presence in a variety of ways.

Another way we draw close is by living our lives in a way that is committed to both the relationship we have with Him and the desire to see His will and purpose fulfilled on the earth. The Bible refers to this a being a living sacrifice:

> *Romans 12:1 – "Therefore, I urge you, brothers and sisters, in view of God's mercy, to offer your bodies as a living* _____, _____ *and* _____ *to God—this is your true and proper worship."*

Another Bible verse tells us that God is actively looking for people whose hearts are fully committed to Him:

> *2 Chronicles 16:9 – "For the eyes of the LORD range throughout the earth to strengthen those whose* _____ *are* _____ *committed to him."*

When we live our lives totally surrendered to our King, we become the living sacrifice that He desires, and His presence actively rests on and around us all the time. Here is another biblical principle for you: fire falls on sacrifice. God will send His presence, His holy fire to be on those who are fully committed to Him. Living life in this way makes it incredibly easy to hear God speaking to us because we are always in a place of closeness to Him. We do not have to schedule a time to praise when we are always in an attitude of praise. Live your life in such a way that it always attracts God's presence. That is a big key to hearing His voice all the time.

Now for some practical application. There are some simple ways to practice listening to God, and over time, you will be able to discern between His voice, your own thoughts, and even the thoughts that the enemy tries to inject into your mind. Take some time right now to sit quietly before the Lord and listen to what He wants to say to you. Here's a tip, God is always speaking, but we are not always listening. Take some time and listen right now, then write down what He says to you.

_____

_____

_____
_____
_____
_____

You can also ask God specific about yourself or about situations in life. Take a few minutes to ask God these questions and write down what He says to you:

What do You think about me?

_____
_____
_____
_____
_____
_____

How do You feel about me?

_____
_____
_____
_____
_____

As you learn to hear His voice, you will begin to realize that there is no limit to the conversations you can have with your Creator. He always has something to say to you. He always has the advice and wisdom that you need. In fact, He has the best advice and wisdom any of us can ever receive. As we journey with the Lord, we need to keep in mind that this is not some simple religion where we memorize the content of a book and regurgitate it for others. This is a relationship with the Creator of the universe, and a relationship will never flourish if we do not have conversations. Our goal is to get to know Him, not just know about Him. We should have the desire to draw close to Him and hear what He has to say. We should have the desire to know Him in such a way that it changes the way we live, the way we interact with others, and the way we view the world around us.

The closer we draw to Him, the more His ideas become our ideas, and the more we view our reality through His eyes. The more we converse, the deeper the conversations become. It is vitally important for every follower of Jesus to know that they can have a conversation with their King. It is vitally important to recognize His voice because, if we are willing to listen, He will keep us on track to fulfill the mission and destiny for which we were created. Never stop listening.

Video Wrap Up – Scan the QR code below to hear some final thoughts from Gene and Lauren about a common question on this topic:

Lesson Twenty-One

Prophecy

The previous lesson laid a foundation for how to hear God's voice, specifically for yourself, but you can also hear what He wants to say to other people. As with the other spiritual gifts covered in previous lessons, the gift of prophecy is listed in 1 Corinthians 12. Different ministers have defined prophecy in different ways, some maybe better than others, but as was defined earlier, the definition we are using is that it is *supernatural information given by Holy Spirit about the future.* As you learned in the previous lesson, there are many different ways God speaks to us, but everything He says is not about the future, so we need to be careful not to define everything we hear from God as prophecy. This lesson focuses on how to hear God's plans for people's lives and how to share what you hear in a healthy manner. Some similar areas of ministry will also be covered at the end of the lesson.

The gift of prophecy is a gift. It is something we receive from Holy Spirit that allows us to share what God is speaking about the future to encourage others. This gift should never be used for manipulation, control, or to judge someone for the direction they are headed. If the gift of prophecy is used for these negative purposes, it is in cooperation with a spirit that is not of God. The Bible gives a very specific framework that a person ministering in the gift of prophecy must stay within in order for the process and prophecy to remain healthy. Anyone operating in the gift of prophecy must stay within this framework:

> *1 Corinthians 14:3- "But the one who prophesies speaks to people for their _____ , _____ and _____ ."*

Sharing with someone what God is saying to them about their future can be very exciting for the person prophesying as well as for the person receiving the message. It releases a strength for them to walk out their God-given mission knowing what is coming. It releases encouragement by showing that God not only cares about the person but also has an actual plan for their life. It releases comfort through the awareness and knowledge that their situation is going to change, their season is going to change, and that there is something more for them just a little ways further down the road.

You can also receive a good word from God for someone that is not prophecy and still share with them what God is speaking. It is very encouraging to hear what the Lord thinks about a person or a particular situation, even if it is not about the future. Everything God speaks is important, and as you continue to hone your ability to hear His voice, you may find that He will use you to speak what He wants to say into other people's lives that has a great impact even without officially prophesying something about the future. Do not ever discount anything God wants to share with someone, even if it seems too simple. It can have impacts greater than any of us may realize at the moment.

Encouraging people with a message from God is great, but there is also a bit of a warning everyone involved in any type of ministry needs to keep in mind. If we do not minister in love, we should not be ministering at all. Love must be the priority in ministry. The goal in prophesying should never be to make ourselves look important or to set ourselves apart from other believers because we have a special gift. The goal is to love people. Take some time right now to read the entire chapter of 1 Corinthians 13, so that you have an understanding of what love looks like in the kingdom of God. Here's the first verse to get you started:

> *1 Corinthians 13:1 – "If I speak in the tongues of men or of angels, but do not have love, I am only a resounding _____ or a clanging _____."*

Because love is so essential, there are two prayers we have regularly prayed for many years, and that we often teach others to pray, as it has a great impact on the way we view everything around us:

1. Help me to see people the way you see them.
2. Help me to love people the way you love them.

When we can see people through the eyes of Jesus, we see them the way He sees them, which is not always what we may see through our natural eyes. When Jesus looks at someone, he does not just see who they are right now, or what they are involved in right now. He sees their potential. He sees their purpose. He sees their divine destiny. When we can see people in this way, we can easily look past anything we consider to be a failure and focus instead on what God's plan is for their life. Every person is created in the image of God, so every person is worthy of honor, regardless of their current situation in life. Love and honor are kingdom principles that should be infused into every type of ministry and interaction.

When studying this topic, people often have questions about the differences between the gift of prophecy and a prophet. The distinction is quite easy once we know the role of a prophet and the role of a person operating in a gifting. As mentioned in an earlier chapter, Ephesians chapter 4 provides us with the primary role of five particular categories of ministers that have a specific calling given to them by Jesus to lead the Church:

> *Ephesians 4:11-13 – "So Christ himself gave the apostles, the _____, the evangelists, the pastors and teachers, to _____ his people for works of service, so that the body of Christ may be built up until we all reach unity in the faith and in the knowledge of the Son of God and become mature, attaining to the whole measure of the fullness of Christ."*

Prophets hear God and prophesy in the same way someone with a gift of prophecy can hear God, but their primary role is to equip other believers. Prophets also operate with a kingdom governmental authority that allows them to, not only teach and train, but also to provide direction, bring correction, and spur action to the church as needed. These elements are not part of the gift of prophecy. When operating in the gift of prophecy, as previously mentioned, a person must stay within the realm of strengthening, encouraging, and comforting. Prophets have the authority from God to do more in this realm because of the specific nature of their calling and anointing. That does not mean that one is more important than the other, it simply means that the role is different.

Taking all of this into account, ministering to someone prophetically, or in an encouraging way that is not prophecy, is very similar to hearing God speak to you personally. Just as you learned to ask God questions about yourself in the previous lesson, you can also ask Him questions about other people.

Here are some great questions you can ask when you want to minister to someone in this way:

- What do you want to say to this person right now?
- What do you want them to see that they are not seeing?
- How do you feel about this person?
- Will you show me something uniquely specific that is just for this person?

These types of questions are great to get the ball rolling and as God begins to speak, our job is to simply repeat what He is saying to us or showing us. As mentioned earlier, you do not need the gift of prophecy to minister in this way. You can encourage someone with something God is speaking without it being about the future. This simple method of asking God questions works great in any type of one-on-one ministry. As you ask God these questions in your mind, and He begins to speak to you, you can speak what He is saying to the person standing in front of you. It really is that simple. The only part that may seem difficult is to learn to hear God clearly and to be willing to take the risk of sharing what you think He is saying. In doing this, there are some common ways we can phrase our statements that comfortably invite the individual into an encounter with God:

- I feel like God is saying ...
- I think the Lord is saying ...
- I think what God is showing me ...

These types of phrases give the person we are ministering to the option of deciding for themselves whether it is a message from God. It is possible that we may get it wrong. It is possible that we may get part of it wrong. It is possible that we may give the person the most profound message they have ever heard. Only they will know if it resonates with their spirit. Even if you have 100% confidence that it is a direct word from the Lord, do not push it on them; let them decide for themselves if they want to receive it. A great question to ask after we have ministered in this way is: does that resonate with you?

Ultimately, the goal is to give someone an encounter with Jesus. If what you say resonates with someone, it will be a great encouragement. If it does not resonate now, it may resonate later, and you should encourage them to hold onto it and see what transpires later. As you mature in this style of ministry, you will find that God will expand how He speaks to you, and it will take on a style that is very unique to your own personality. Putting these foundational principles into practice is just the beginning.

Take a moment to ask God to release this gift into your life and write down what you experience:

_____
_____
_____
_____
_____
_____

Return to this space in a few weeks to record any prophetic words you have received and what happened after you shared them with someone:

_____
_____
_____
_____
_____
_____

Video Wrap Up – Scan the QR code below to hear some final thoughts from Gene and Lauren about a common question on this topic:

Lesson Twenty-Two

Miracles and Faith

It is fun to read and study about the miracles Jesus performed during the time He ministered on the earth. As we read these testimonies in Scripture, we can see that there were times He healed sick people by taking away diseases, and there were times the healing involved the creation of a capability that did not previously exist, such as giving sight to a man who was born blind. On one hand, we could say that all supernatural healings are miraculous, but the Bible draws a distinction between healings and miracles, especially when we read about the gifts of the Spirit.

Some things are easy to categorize as miracles, such as when Jesus turned water into wine or caused food to multiply and feed thousands of people as we see in John chapters 2 and 6. But when it comes to the physical body, the line between healing and miracles can be a bit blurred. Where that line is drawn is not of huge significance, but it is good to draw it somewhere, so we have a distinction. Healings are typically categorized as sickness and disease leaving the body, while miracles are categorized as a major change occurring in the function of the body. For example, if someone who has a bad fever suddenly does not have a fever anymore, we could categorize that as healing. If a bone grows back, or a broken spine is suddenly repaired, that would be better categorized as a miracle.

Miracles typically involve matter coming into existence or a change occurring at an atomic level. Take for instance the miracle of a person whose leg supernaturally grew two inches to match the length of the other leg. Think about what would have to happen for this to occur. The bone would certainly need to grow two inches. So would the skin, and the blood vessels, and the muscle, and the nerves, and everything else that functions as part of the leg. Even hair follicles would have to form on the newly grown skin. How could this be possible? Where did all the substances to cause all these parts of the leg come from? The only explanation is that those atoms that formed the new part of the leg came into existence when the miracle occurred.

Even the account of the cursed fig tree in Matthew 18 was miraculous because the cells that formed the tree immediately began dying causing the tree to wither. If we go further back into the Old Testament, to 2 Kings 6, we see a miracle of an axe head floating to the top of the water. The atomic structure of the axe head did not seem to change, but somehow the buoyancy of the water changed in such a way that the axe head floated to the top. So, what we see in the realm of miracles is that changes are made at atomic levels, or the laws of nature are temporarily changed to allow something unordinary to take place.

The gift of working miracles may require more faith because of the nature of the miracle itself. As a new believer, you may struggle with the idea of seeing someone supernaturally healed, but after you have seen it occur a few times, your faith will grow to cause you to see healing occur more frequently. The same is true of miracles. It may be hard for you to imagine a new kidney being placed inside someone's body, but if you see it happen, it will increase your faith to see similar types of miracles take place as well. You do not necessarily need the gift of faith to see a miracle take place, but those who are operating in a gift of faith are probably more likely to see greater miracles take place. Take a moment to think about the types of miracles you would like to see occur and list them here:

_____

_____

_____

_____

The gift of faith is different from the type of faith we tend to grow in as we partner with God in supernatural activities. The gift of faith is something supernaturally deposited in us, usually for a specific event or action. It is not typically something that is stirred up within us as we see other miraculous things happening around us. It is a different type of faith altogether. Some have said that when you operate with a gift of faith, anything you say will happen. This is because in this situation you are operating with a supernatural faith that is much greater than any other type of faith.

One catalyst for operating in a gift of faith is a word of knowledge. Some words of knowledge are so pronounced that the person receiving them also receives a great measure of supernatural faith at that moment to declare that healing is going to immediately take place. Normally, as you learned in an earlier lesson, we share words of knowledge and then watch to see what God does. But a word of knowledge that comes with a gift of faith is different because you suddenly know with zero doubt that a miracle is about to occur at that very moment.

A gift of faith can also manifest in other ways apart from other spiritual gifts. Elijah seemed to be operating with a supernatural faith in 1 Kings 18 when he gathered together the priests of Baal for a challenge to see who the one true God really was. He taunted them as they performed their ceremonies in such a way that he must have already known what was about to happen. The faith he had in this situation was so great that it is unlikely to have been anything other than supernatural faith for the moment at hand:

> *1 Kings 18:37-38 – "Then the fire of the Lord _____ and burned up the sacrifice, the wood, the stones and the soil, and also licked up the water in the trench."*

The gift of faith is the faith to believe anything can happen. It can be connected to miracles taking place in the body or in nature. It can even be such that the person operating in the gift can speak something into existence or cause something to be removed. Jesus spoke of a type of faith that could cause a mountain to be moved:

> *Matthew 17:20 – "Truly I tell you, if you have _____ as small as a mustard seed, you can say to this mountain, 'Move from here to there,' and it will move. _____ will be impossible for you."*

Consider that if a mustard seed level of faith could do this, what could a supernatural gift of faith bring about? There really is no impossibility when Holy Spirit empowers you in the many different ways that He uses to bring about His kingdom on the earth.

Take a moment to ask God to release these gifts into your life and write down what you experience:

_____

_____

_____

_____

_____

_____

Return to this space in a few weeks to record any miracles or gifts of faith you have experienced since praying this prayer:

_____

_____

_____

_____

_____

_____

Video Wrap Up – Scan the QR code below to hear some final thoughts from Gene and Lauren about a common question on this topic:

Lesson Twenty-Three

Tongues and Interpretation

Speaking in tongues, like all the other gifts of the Spirit, is mysterious, but it tends to stand out from the rest of the gifts because it is designed to be used more frequently by believers as a personal prayer language on a daily basis as well as to give a public message to the church. The gift of speaking in tongues is sometimes the first gift a follower of Jesus receives when filled with the Holy Spirit, but this is not always the case. Holy Spirit gets to decide what gifts He distributes, who He gives them to, and when they are given.

> *1 Corinthians 12:11 – "All these are the work of one and the same Spirit, and he distributes them to each one, just as he _____."*

As an individual prayer language, praying in tongues is a powerful way to connect with God without thinking about what you are saying or simply going through a list of items you want to pray about. Praying in this way enables us to pray directly to God in a language that only He knows and understands. Sometimes we are not sure how to pray, and in those moments, praying in tongues is the best thing we can do. Sometimes we have a deep desire to praise God in a way that human words cannot suffice, causing us to sing out in this heavenly language. As we pray and worship in tongues, we are speaking to the King of the universe in a way that may sound crazy to others, but he understands perfectly.

> *1 Corinthians 14:2 – "For anyone who speaks in a _____ does not speak to people but to _____. Indeed, no one understands them; they utter mysteries by the Spirit."*

When the Apostle Paul discussed this gift, he specifically highlighted the fact that praying in tongues edifies or builds up the individual doing the praying. This gift is, essentially, Holy Spirit praying through you. If Holy Spirit is praying through you, then what you pray is always in line with the will of God. You may not know what you are saying, but it works like a tool that builds and strengthens you to live out your life as a greater witness and testimony of the Lord. The more time someone spends praying in this personal prayer language, the more they will be built up, and the language itself will grow as the gift is used.

> *1 Corinthians 14:4 – "Anyone who speaks in a tongue edifies _____ ..."*

In addition to a personal prayer language, praying in tongues is also a powerful way to pray for other people. Praying for someone else is known as intercession, it is the act of a person interceding on behalf of someone else before the throne of God, and it is a very common thing within the body of Christ to pray for each other. Like personal prayer, we do not always know how to pray for another person's situation. Sometimes we know that they need healing or a particular type of breakthrough, but when we are unsure how to pray, pulling tongues off our spiritual gifts tool belt is the way to go. There have been numerous testimonies of healing, breakthrough, deliverance from addiction, and other major miraculous things occurring because of praying or interceding in tongues.

Sometimes Holy Spirit will deliver a message publicly to a body of believers by speaking a message in tongues through a particular individual. This is different from a personal prayer language or intercession. This is very common in some church congregations and less in others today, but it does occur from time to time. In these instances, Scripture tells us that the person used in this way should ask Holy Spirit for the interpretation so that the entire body can be built up by what Holy Spirit is speaking.

> *1 Corinthians 14:13 – "...one who speaks in a tongue should pray that they may _____ what they say."*

Interpreting a gift of tongues is the final gift of the Spirit to be discussed and is, obviously, closely tied to speaking in tongues. There is typically only one way this gift is used, and that is when a public message is given in tongues. Holy Spirit can, of course, give you an interpretation of anything you pray in tongues, or what others are praying in tongues, so it is wise not to limit how He wants to use us based on personal experiences or historical accounts. When an interpretation is given, it sounds a lot like a prophetic word and carries more weight than a tongue that is not interpreted because it builds up the body of believers.

> *1 Corinthians 14:5 – "The one who prophesies is greater than the one who speaks in tongues, unless someone _____, so that the church may be edified."*

In the very first account of speaking in tongues, which is found in Acts chapter 2, the visitors in town who heard the disciples speaking wondered how it was possible that a group of Jews could be speaking in languages from other nations. There are 15 different cities, nations, or regions listed in this chapter, which means that 15 different languages were probably being spoken by the disciples of Jesus. This raises the question of whether speaking in tongues is an earthly language we do not know or a heavenly language that is known only to God. The answer is that it appears to be both, and Holy Spirit may use us differently depending on what He wants to accomplish.

There have been many accounts of people who, while praying in tongues, were unknowingly praying perfectly in another human language they have never learned. At the same time, someone else present in the room, who knew that language, could understand what the person was praying. These situations have led people to give their lives to Jesus because of what was being prayed and because of their witnessing of this supernatural type of prayer. It is an incredible thing to see the creativity of the Holy Spirit at work, even in these rare instances.

Take a few minutes right now and ask God to give you the gift of speaking in tongues. It is something every follower of Jesus should ask for because it is a gift that we can use every single day to be built up and to pray in line with the will of God for any situation we encounter in life. Ask Him now, and write down what happens:

_____
_____
_____
_____
_____
_____

Video Wrap Up – Scan the QR code below to hear some final thoughts from Gene and Lauren about a common question on this topic:

Lesson Twenty-Four

Constant Pursuit

The life of following Jesus is one that brings a spiritual maturity over time, much like that in the physical world. As children, we mature over time as we learn about our environment, how to live in a family and society, attend schools, and are influenced by everything around us. No one wants to stay a toddler all their lives. Every teenager wants to move out of their parents' house, spread their wings, and start out on the adventure of all that awaits them in life. As humans, we crave the maturation process up to a certain point, and then we need to make decisions about the direction we want to go and what that direction requires of us.

Following Jesus is very similar in the respect that we need to mature in our faith. There are many things you will learn as a new believer that you will also need to experience over time before the truth of what you learned completely takes hold. The Bible is full of mysteries that can only be fully explained through a revelation from Holy Spirit, and as such, reading a thousand books on the topic will never bring about a full understanding. Following Jesus is an experiential relationship that will take you on spiritual journeys you could never experience without Him; the more time you spend with Him, the greater the journey and revelation of His truth.

Because this is an experiential relationship, you will need to be intentional about setting aside time to spend with Jesus. We have said this already, but it is worth repeating. Just like any human relationship, it will grow as you spend time with Him. You would never enter a human relationship, talk to that person once every few weeks, and expect the relationship to flourish. Relationships grow over time as you spend time with someone on a regular basis. The more time you spend with Him, the more you will receive from the relationship, the more you will get to know His personality, His perspective on things, and receive specific direction for your life. You learned in an earlier lesson that God wants to spend time with you, but in most situations, He is waiting for you to show up. Put in the time and you will reap a huge reward.

Jeremiah 29:13 – "You will seek me and _____ me when you seek me with all your heart."

This lifestyle is one of constant pursuit and growth, but it is easy to level off and plateau if you allow yourself to settle into a comfortable routine that does not continuously stretch you to grow spiritually. Many followers of Jesus plateau early in their relationships and do not even know they have stopped growing. It is easy to get into a weekly church attendance routine, read the Bible for a few minutes each day, and "check the box" of being a Christian that does not require us to pursue everything God has for each one of us. Every believer needs to be in a place of the constant pursuit for more of God.

It is important to remember that God always has more for you. There is always more of Him to discover. No matter how many experiences you have with Him, how often you have felt His presence or heard His voice, there is always something new available to you. We can spend all of eternity with Him and still not know all there is to know about Him. We can spend thousands of years learning directly from His voice and still have so much more to learn. This is the greatest adventure and the greatest relationship you will ever have the privilege of participating in; a relationship with the One who spoke everything into existence!

As a new follower of Jesus, you are in a phase where you are learning the basics about the identity God has given to you, about who He is, and about the mission He has for you on this planet. As you spend time with Him, ask specific questions about your life's calling. Here are a few to get you started:

What have you created me to accomplish?

_____

_____

_____

_____

_____

What do I need to learn to fulfill my purpose?

_____

_____

_____

_____

_____

What should I be doing in this current season of my life?

_____

_____

_____

_____

_____

The answers to these questions are usually part of your journey. You will discover more layers to your personal calling as you move forward in life and God will reveal more to you over time as you continue in your relationship with Him. Your assignment in different seasons of life will change; learn to go with the flow of what the Holy Spirit wants you to do. You can do OK in life by following Jesus, but you will thrive when you are exactly where He wants you. Always pursue what He wants, learn to follow His direction, and He will never steer you wrong.

Here are some simple, practical tips to help you in your constant pursuit of more of Jesus:

- Never be satisfied, stay hungry for more, even after every great experience, still go for more!
- Ask Him to use you in a way that causes His kingdom to come to earth to transform the culture of the world around you.
- Set aside every personal desire and replace it with what He wants; what He wants is always more important than anything else.
- He is your King, and His perspective will always be better than any perspective in the world. Always ask for His perspective on everything.
- Do not let what you do become your identity. Your identity is never in a title or position; it is always in Him.
- Do not let mistakes hold you back. Everyone makes mistakes, but we do not need to let them define us or affect our future.

Video Wrap Up – Scan the QR code below to hear some final thoughts from Gene and Lauren about a common question on this topic:

Lesson Twenty-Five

The Need for Community

When you chose to follow Jesus, in a sense, you joined a new family. Every person who follows Jesus is part of this family, also called the body of Christ. Everyone within the body of Christ has a purpose and role assigned by Jesus that enables the body to function in a manner that allows His mission to be fulfilled on earth. It is important for this body to function in a healthy manner that brings honor to Jesus and each other while we work together to make the world a better place. Your role is an important one, even if you have not figured out what it is yet! But your role is not more or less important than other members of the body. Keeping this in mind will help us to avoid division and conflict over trivial matters.

> *1 Corinthians 12:25-27: "...so that there should be no division in the body, but that its parts should have equal concern for each other. If one part suffers, every part suffers with it; if one part is honored, every part rejoices with it. Now you are the _____ of Christ, and each one of you is a _____ of it."*

For the body to function healthily, we need to stay connected to a community of believers who can walk alongside us in our journey. This is especially important for new believers so you can become well-grounded in your faith and have a solid foundation to build upon as you continue to follow Jesus throughout your life. This does not mean we need to live in the same neighborhood or isolate ourselves away from the rest of society, but it means we need to be intentional about having healthy Christian relationships with people we see on a regular basis.

Living in community allows us to be accountable to each other in the way we live our lives. It is incredibly helpful to have someone who can encourage you when you are not in the best frame of mind, give you guidance and wisdom when you are faced with tough decisions, and help you to overcome the many different challenges that you will encounter in life. You are going to have questions. You are going to wonder about the many different things you read about in the Bible. Having a seasoned Christian in your life who can answer those questions and point you in the right direction is not only helpful but also very important. Solomon summed it up in this way:

Proverbs 27:17 – "As iron _____ iron, so one person _____ another."

We sharpen each other when we spend time discussing the ways of God within a healthy community of Jesus lovers. A common place we find this community is within a local church. It is best to find one that believes in the full gospel of Jesus, has not adopted the belief that the gifts of the Spirit have ceased, and whose leaders teach and live according to the word of God without compromising their beliefs to appease others who may feel uncomfortable with the truth of the gospel. The principles of the kingdom, some of which you have discovered in the preceding lessons, can be offensive to people who have adopted the world's viewpoint. As followers of Jesus, we submit to our

King first. Many local churches tend to have slightly different perspectives on more trivial matters that are not central to the gospel, but the church you choose should at least have a solid belief in the core elements. Trust Holy Spirit in this decision and, the more time you spend with Him, the more easily you will be able to recognize if a church is healthy.

On the note of healthy churches, not all churches meet in traditional buildings or operate as large gatherings. Historically, followers of Jesus met in homes long before they were meeting in formalized church buildings. There are pros and cons to both, but do not assume that a larger church is better than a small one, or that a house church is less valuable than a megachurch. It is incredible to stand in a large room with thousands of other people worshipping Jesus together. It is also incredible to be amongst a handful of believers worshipping Jesus together in a living room. Find somewhere that loves to worship Jesus, goes deep into the Scriptures, and equips you for your mission on earth.

As you continue your journey you will find it very valuable to have spiritual leaders in your life who have walked with the Lord for a long time and who can give you sound advice. Natural parents take on this role for their children, and of course, as children become teenagers, they tend to stop listening to their parents because they think they know everything. As we get older, we realize how important it is to have others speak wisdom into our life. Within the realm of the church, these spiritual leaders become like spiritual parents. It is healthy to have wise leaders you can regularly spend time with, who can answer your questions, and keep you pointed in the right direction. Sometimes this is the pastor of the church you attend. Sometimes it is a friend who lives down the street from you. Holy Spirit will bring the right person to fill this role in your life, trust His guidance and trust the one He sends to you.

Healthy leaders can mentor you and give you feedback on what you think God is saying to keep you on the right track.

169

Often a new believer struggles with hearing the voice of God because it is a new concept and they have not yet practiced listening to the point where they can be sure how to discern when God is speaking to them or when it is their own thoughts. Having someone who can confirm for you what you believe God is saying, or let you know that it is not God is very valuable, not just as a new follower of Jesus, but also throughout your entire life. Seek out those who can give you wisdom and help you discern what you are hearing.

Some leaders in the body of Christ fall into a group generally referred to as the five-fold ministry. This name comes from a passage of Scripture where we are told there are five positions Jesus created to function as leaders within the body. These are apostles, prophets, evangelists, pastors, and teachers. There are many other roles within the body, but those God has called into these specific leadership roles are charged with the responsibility to equip followers of Jesus to fulfill their mission on the earth:

> Ephesians 4:11-13 – "So Christ himself gave the
> _____, the _____, the _____, the
> _____ and _____, to equip his people for
> works of service, so that the body of Christ may be built
> up until we all reach unity in the faith and in the
> knowledge of the Son of God and become mature,
> attaining to the whole measure of the fullness of Christ."

These are not titles or positions we give ourselves, though some people have done so in the past. These are callings that God puts on people's lives, and only He can decide a person's role within His kingdom. Pastors have been the most common role that believers have encountered within the church in the past few hundred years, but more recently there has been a resurgence of people stepping into their God-given positions in the other areas of the five-fold ministry. This is not to say that those positions were ever done away with by God, but that some theological viewpoints chose not to include them within their construct for various reasons. Every follower of Jesus is part of the body of Christ, and as such, we should remember that one is not better than the other and one should not be excluded because we do not understand their gift or calling.

Our gifts and callings should be used to complete each other, not to compete with each other. If you look at all the different denominations of the church on the earth today, you may think that this statement about competition is untrue. Sadly, some denominations were birthed out of disagreements among members of the body of Christ, and it can make it feel like there is competition at times. Any organization of people will have disagreements and conflicts over varying issues. But, if we live our lives with an understanding that each of our individual purposes can be used to serve each other, as we also serve Christ, the conflicts can be more easily avoided or resolved. This is another reason why love, which you learned about in an earlier lesson, is such a vital component of God's kingdom.

Take a few minutes to think about what element of a healthy community is missing from your life right now, or was previously missing from your life, and write them down here:

_____
_____
_____
_____
_____

Now, take a few more minutes to think about what a healthy community of believers can provide you personally and write them down here:

_____
_____
_____

All people need a community to live a healthy life. It is unhealthy to be alone or to be in environments that do not encourage you to grow. Followers of Jesus who do not spend time in a healthy Christian community tend to develop unbalanced or incorrect positions on the Bible and the Christian lifestyle. Being in a healthy community of believers keeps this from happening, stretches you to grow closer to Jesus, and provides you with an appropriate level of accountability. Pursuing these healthy community relationships will help you to stay in sync with what God is doing and keep you moving in the right direction.

Video Wrap Up – Scan the QR code below to hear some final thoughts from Gene and Lauren about a common question on this topic:

Lesson Twenty-Six

Baptism and Communion

A hallmark of the beginning of the ministry of Jesus was when He was baptized in water by John the Baptist. Water baptism is symbolic of the death, burial, and resurrection of Jesus. When a believer is baptized in water, it is a public declaration of their choice to follow Jesus, and it is symbolic of their own death and resurrection with Christ. It is more than simple tradition; it is an outward expression of your inward faith in Jesus and your desire to follow Him completely. It is also a command of Jesus that all believers should be baptized:

> *Matt 28:18 – "...go and make disciples of all nations,*
> _____ *them in the name of the Father and of the*
> *Son and of the Holy Spirit..."*

Different denominations of Christianity handle baptism in different ways. Some practice baptisms by pouring water over a person's head, others sprinkle water onto the person, and some submerge people fully underwater in a large tank or container and then bring them back up out of the water. What we see in the account of Jesus' baptism is that He came up out of the water, which means He must have been under the water before coming out. This is what is called baptism by immersion. Every other example in the Bible that describes a baptism event is described in this same way, making baptism by immersion the most common method used in the Bible. This may not be practical in all situations. Someone with a physical disability may not be able to be immersed in water. It would be silly to say that not being immersed does not count as baptism. We prefer total immersion but be careful not to create a theology out of the process.

> *Acts 8:38-39 "He ordered the carriage to stop, and they went down into the water, and Philip baptized him. When they came up _____ of the water, the Spirit of the Lord snatched Philip away..."*

Baptism should only be done after a person has given their life to Jesus and generally understands what it means to follow Jesus. Parents of young children who choose to follow Jesus should wait until the child is an appropriate age, which can be different for everyone, where they have this general understating, otherwise, it is just another religious practice with little meaning for the child. The practice of infant baptism is never discussed in Scripture and is not in line with any example within Scripture, likely because an infant cannot make a willful determination for themselves to follow Jesus or understand what baptism means. It would be good for someone who was baptized as an infant and later chooses to follow Jesus, to be baptized again.

Baptism is also not a requirement for salvation. There are many people who get saved later in life and die before ever having the chance to be baptized. The Bible does not stipulate that baptism is part of salvation, but it is a command given by Jesus that every believer should follow if the opportunity is available. In this way, we follow the example of our Lord and show that we desire to live a life fully dead to the things of the world and fully alive to the things of the Spirit:

> *Romans 6:4-11 – "We were therefore buried with him through _____ into death..."*

So, baptism by water is both an act of obedience and a public declaration of faith. It is an exhilarating moment for a new Christian, and many have described profound spiritual encounters that have taken place during this event. Typically, this is something you only do once during your life, though sometimes people will be baptized again when visiting significant biblical regions such as the Jordan river in Israel where Jesus was baptized. If you have not yet been baptized, talk to your pastor about it and take the time to follow Jesus' example in this way.

Communion is another practice within the Christian faith that should be observed on a regular basis. When Jesus ate the last supper with His disciples, He described communion in this way:

> *Matthew 26:26-28 – "While they were eating, Jesus took bread, and when he had given thanks, he broke it and gave it to his disciples, saying, "Take and eat; this is my body." Then he took a cup, and when he had given thanks, he gave it to them, saying, "Drink from it, all of you. This is my blood of the covenant, which is poured out for many for the forgiveness of sins."*

You can easily see the symbolism in this passage. The bread represents the body of Jesus that was broken for us and the wine, or grape juice in many churches, represents the blood of Jesus that was shed for our forgiveness. When we partake of communion, we are doing it as an act of remembrance of what He did for us, as well as an act of faith that everything He paid for is available to us today. As with baptism, there are different customs for how communion is taken. And also like baptism, this is mostly based on tradition and sometimes due to different interpretations of Scripture.

What this typically looks like is some form of bread and wine, or grape juice, is distributed to everyone in the room, a leader prays a prayer of thankfulness to Jesus for His sacrifice for our sins, for bringing us into His kingdom, and for our opportunity to serve Him. People are then invited to eat the bread and drink the wine as they individually remember how Jesus transformed their lives. It is a solemn moment as well as a celebratory one. It is not a time to remember all the mistakes we have made in our past, but to know that His sacrifice wiped away everything.

Some church traditions observe communion on one particular Sunday each month and on other special occasions throughout the year. Other churches take communion every single week. Some view communion as so sacred that a priest or pastor must oversee the observance and personally provide the elements to each individual. Others take communion frequently in their own homes as a way to remember what Jesus did for them as they spend time with the Lord each day. It is important not to make a theology out of these different traditions The Bible tells us to take communion in remembrance of Jesus; that is the key piece. It should be a regular practice in your life and serve as a reminder of what Christ paid for your soul on the cross. Any practice that keeps us focused on Him is a good thing.

If you have not yet been baptized, we encourage you to contact your pastor and schedule a time to participate in this holy exercise of publicly declaring your faith.

Video Wrap Up – Scan the QR code below to hear some final thoughts from Gene and Lauren about a common question on this topic:

Lesson Twenty-Seven

Fasting

If you spend any time around Christians, you will at some point encounter someone who is fasting for a period of time. Traditional fasting is the act of giving up food for a period of time and replacing the time you would normally eat with prayer, worship, and focused devotion to God. People who fast for a whole day, or for longer periods, also typically spend more time praying throughout the day and not just during mealtime. Fasting has been described and defined in many ways, but the simplest way is to think about it is in terms of a relationship.

Couples in a relationship will often take time out of their schedules to spend time just with each other. Taking a trip for a day or two to another location can be very beneficial for couples because they separate themselves away from work, children, things that need to be done around the house, and other daily requirements or distractions, for the purpose of focusing on each other. This is the core of what fasting is really about. It is the act of separating yourself from something your physical body needs each day in order to focus that time on Jesus. Working on a relationship costs something. It can cost time, money, and resources, to develop and grow a healthy relationship. Fasting is one of the ways that we invest in our relationship with God.

One of your primary goals as a follower of Jesus is to know Him more. Not just know about Him, but really know Him. The only way we can do this is by intentionally setting aside time and space to spend time with Him. We have said that multiple times already throughout this book. Your normal daily routine of prayer, worship, and reading the Bible is the number one way to spend time with Him. Fasting takes it to another level. When we intentionally give something up for the purpose of spending more time with Jesus, we are declaring that nothing is more important than Him and that we desire to be with Him so much that we will give up other things in life so we can grow closer to our King. Even Jesus fasted, at least one time, as He prepared to enter full-time ministry:

Luke 4:1-2 – "Jesus, full of the Holy Spirit, left the Jordan and was led by the Spirit into the wilderness, where for forty days he was tempted by the devil. He ate _____ during those days, and at the end of them he was hungry."

Fasting does not have to be just about food, but food is the thing most people think about when they hear the word fasting. You can also fast other things that you tend to spend time on each day and insert Jesus into that time instead. Television is a good example of something that you can fast in this way, especially because it is good to disconnect from entertainment and other voices when we want to hear God more clearly. In fact, there are times when God will tell you to fast a particular thing for a season of time. Pay attention to His leading because when He asks this of you, it is to take you into a deeper relationship with Him.

Fasting empties of ourselves so that we can be postured to be filled with more of Him. It is not a logical practice from a human perspective. It does not make sense to our human minds that giving up food for a few days can somehow bring about a supernatural result. It only makes sense if you look at it from a spiritual perspective. God established this principle and created a method for us to practice sacrificing a small but significant thing as another way of worshipping and honoring Him. There are several different purposes for which people fasted in the Bible and each one goes back to the root of seeking God for something deeper:

To seek direction, guidance, or protection

> *Judges 20:26-28 – "They _____ that day until evening...They asked, 'Shall we go up again to fight against the Benjamites, our fellow Israelites, or not?'"*

> *2 Chronicles 20:3 – "Jehoshaphat resolved to _____ of the Lord, and he proclaimed a fast for all Judah."*

To repent

> *1 Samuel 7:6 – "On that day they fasted and there they _____, 'We have sinned against the Lord.'"*

To worship

> *Luke 2:37 – "She never left the temple but _____ night and day, _____ and praying."*

To bring freedom

> *Isaiah 58:6 – "Is not this the kind of _____ I have chosen: to loose the chains of injustice and untie the*

cords of the yoke, to set the oppressed _____ and break every yoke?"

Matthew 17:21 – "But this kind does not go out except by prayer and _____."

As you can see from these verses, people have fasted for thousands of years to intentionally seek the face of God for many different reasons. When we are intentional about fasting, we are living a lifestyle that loudly declares God is more important to us than anything else. As you grow as a believer you will begin to recognize more and more how important it is to keep God above everything else. Fasting is a great way to put that into practice on a regular basis. Start small and you will grow into it.

Some people fast one or two days every week, or at the beginning of each year to seek direction for the upcoming year. Some fast during the time leading up to Easter, or at different times throughout the year as they feel the need to go deeper. The Bible includes 40-day fasts of all food, 21-day fasts of just eating vegetables, one-day fasts of no food or water, and many others without detailed descriptions. You are encouraged to start thinking about fasting now and ask God if there is anything specific He wants you to fast for a period of time.

Take time now and decide when you want to start your first fast and write it here:

_____

Now write down what you are going to fast:

_____

Great, you have a plan for your first fast! As you grow closer to Him, you will want to spend even more time with Him, and fasting on a regular basis will become a normal part of your life. And don't forget that fasting has one great side effect of losing weight, which is not so bad either!

Video Wrap Up – Scan the QR code below to hear some final thoughts from Gene and Lauren about a common question on this topic:

Impartation

In Numbers chapter 11 while the Israelites were traveling to the promised land Moses became overwhelmed with leading such a large number of people, and when he cried out for help, God presented an interesting solution. He told Moses that He would take some of the power of the Spirit that rested on Moses, and distribute it to seventy elders from the tribes:

> *Numbers 11:17 – "I will come down and speak with you there, and I will take some of the power of the Spirit that is on _____ and put it on _____ ."*

This was the first mention of this idea of impartation in the Bible, and later in the New Testament, we see Paul mention this concept of impartation on several occasions. He tells the Roman believers that he wants to come see them, so he can impart a spiritual gift that would make them strong. We also see in Acts that the Holy Spirit fell when Peter and John laid their hands on the people. There is something about praying for others to receive what God has given you that attracts Holy Spirit to a person in a new way. Paul specifically instructed Timothy to stir up the gifts of God that were in him because of the laying on of hands:

Romans 1:11 – "I long to see you so that I may
_____ *to you some spiritual gift to make you*
strong..."

Acts 8:17 – "Then Peter and John placed their hands on
them, and they _____ *the Holy Spirit."*

2 Timothy 1:6 – "For this reason I remind you to fan
into flame the gift of God, which is in you through the
_____ *on of my hands."*

We know for certain that our Father loves to give good
gifts away to His people. Sometimes this is in the form of
spiritual gifts, other times it is particular skills or talents that will
benefit the kingdom. What we see in this story of Moses, and
what seems to be apparent with Paul, is that God often honors
the prayers of His saints by imparting to others what He has
also given to them. This is one of the ways His kingdom
continues to expand on the earth by empowering His followers
to do what He did and even greater things.

John 14:12 – "Very truly I tell you, whoever believes in
me will do the _____ *I have been doing, and they*
will do even _____ *things than these..."*

Humans cannot give spiritual gifts, that is the job of the
Holy Spirit. But the Holy Spirit also does not want these gifts to
be locked up in just a few believers. Just as He used Moses,
Paul, Peter, and John, He continues to use leaders today to stir
up, and impart spiritual gifts so that others can be used in the
full capacity for which they were created. Many people have
received great breakthroughs, increases in the gifts of the Spirit,
and watched God escalate the works of the Holy Spirit within
their lives after simple impartation prayers.

It is a great joy to pray an impartation prayer over anyone who is hungry for more of God, and so we end this book with a prayer for you, that you would encounter the greater things of God in your life and be used powerfully by Him as you serve out His purpose for your life on the earth:

> Jesus, we thank you for all that you have done in, and through us, and we thank you for the awesome privilege and opportunity to carry your presence and steward the gifts that you have given to us. Our prayer is that you would stir up within every reader of this book the desire to know you, not just to know about you. We ask you to give them an insatiable hunger and unquenchable thirst for Your holy presence. We pray, Father, that you would cause Your face to shine upon them and that you would cause every purpose and destiny they were created for to be fulfilled in their lifetime. And we pray that you would impart everything you have given us, to them. Just as you took from what was on Moses, we pray that you would also take from what you have placed on our lives and release it into their lives today. We ask for a complete transference of the anointing to rest upon them in a mighty way so that they can be used to bring your kingdom to earth with signs and wonders following them everywhere they go. Let the sick be healed, lives be restored, and demons run and hide when they show up, so that you would receive everything you paid for on the cross. Amen.

About Gene and Lauren Lloyd

Gene and Lauren Lloyd, co-directors of Wounded No More, serve the social and spiritual needs of Washington D.C.'s impoverished communities through supernatural ministry and equipping believers to partner with Jesus to bring the fullness of his kingdom to earth. They are dedicated to giving back and have spent decades serving others; Lauren as a leader in non-profits advocating for the needs of veterans, military families, and those in underserved populations and Gene, as a twenty-year military veteran and community leader. Whether they are serving on the streets, or teaching in ministry schools and churches, Gene and Lauren combine biblical truths with practical application and empower people to know their true identity and purpose.

Other Books by Gene Lloyd

Normal: The Supernatural Life you were Created to Live

www.ingramcontent.com/pod-product-compliance
Lightning Source LLC
LaVergne TN
LVHW052025080426
835513LV00018B/2166